NORTHWICH AND AROUND AT WORK

PEOPLE AND INDUSTRIES THROUGH THE YEARS

PAUL HURLEY & ROSE HURLEY

AMBERLEY

ACKNOWLEDGEMENTS

The sources for the images and related materials are provided when known. Most of the photographs are from the author's archives. Also, thanks to our commissioning editor, Nick Grant, and Marcus Pennington for their help and advice.

First published 2026

Amberley Publishing
The Hill, Stroud
Gloucestershire, GL5 4EP

www.amberley-books.com

ISBN 978 1 3981 2714 2 (print)
ISBN 978 1 3981 2715 9 (ebook)

British Library Cataloguing in Publication Data.
A catalogue record for this book is available from the British Library.

Origination by Amberley Publishing.
Printed in the UK.

Appointed GPSR EU Representative: Easy Access System Europe Oü, 16879218
Address: Mustamäe tee 50, 10621, Tallinn, Estonia
Contact Details: gpsr.requests@easproject.com, +358 40 500 3575

CONTENTS

INTRODUCTION

The known history of Northwich begins in 1483, when King Richard III granted the manor and village of Northwich to Lord Stanley and his brother Sir George Stanley. The manor remained in the Stanley family until 1784, when the Earl of Derby sold it to John Mort. Later, it became the property of John Pemberton Heywood of Liverpool, who sold the manor, and everything associated with it, including fairs and markets, to the Northwich Local Board.

However, in those far-off days, Northwich consisted mainly of the High Street. Evidence of this is that the small road next to McDonald's is still called Boundary Street. Then from the Dane Bridge along High Street to Crown Street, into Witton Street and onwards, the area was called Witton cum Twambrooks. From the Bullring/High Street and across the Dane Bridge towards and bordering Davenham was the area called Leftwich. Then, from the Town Bridge, you would be in the areas called Castle and Winnington.

By 1956, the Northwich Parliamentary Constituency consisted of the Urban District of Northwich and the Rural District of Northwich, including part of the Rural District of Tarvin. The long-standing MP was Sir John Foster QC.

There were the two riverside firms of Yarwood's and Pimblott's, both shipbuilders, but despite being on a river, they both provided tugs, ferries, barges and small warships for use around the globe. One of the notable people to work at Yarwood's was Thomas Edward Lawrence, better known as Lawrence of Arabia, who worked on the design of the RAF rescue launch *Aquarius*. It was built there to rescue downed pilots. In 1921, he was a full colonel and adviser to Winston Churchill. In 1922, he tried to enlist as an aircraftman in the RAF using a false name, but his past rank was discovered. He was later allowed to join, was exposed again, and joined the Royal Tank Corps again under a false name. Later, he was allowed into the RAF as a humble aircraftman. His life was a roller coaster. He later came to Yarwood's to work on an RAF air sea rescue boat and died in 1935 due to a motorbike accident.

Northwich is famous for the spectacular subsidences that occurred in the late 1800s and early 1900s. They were caused by wild brine pumping and salt mining, resulting in the Northwich buildings subsiding and simply sinking into the earth. When demolished due to the damage caused, buildings were rebuilt on steel girders, allowing them to be jacked up and easily levelled again after subsiding. Some of the new buildings enhanced the town's

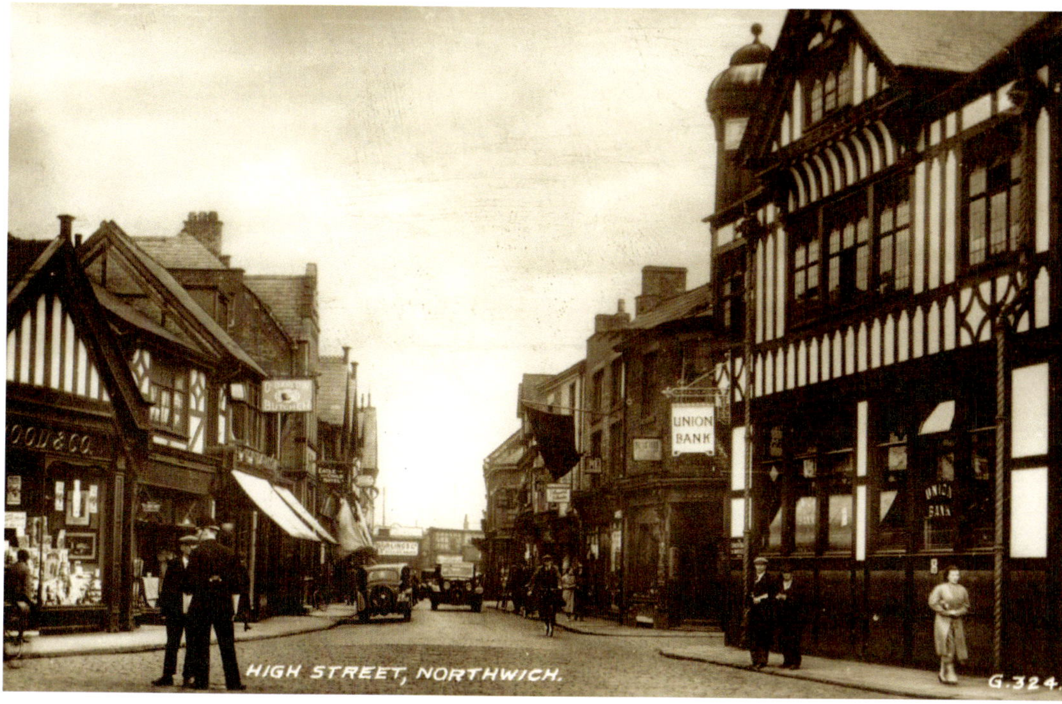

Northwich High Street, c. 1930s.

appearance, including the post office, now a Wetherspoon's pub, and the library, built in the mock-Tudor or Cheshire black-and-white style. The library is a building now showing signs of wear and has closed pending work to address the problems.

This is a brief look at Northwich through the ages, starting with salt and then soda ash. The Lion Salt Works is a restored historic open-pan salt-making site that is now open to the public at Marston, near Northwich, and the old Workhouse, later the Salt Museum, is now the Weaver Hall Museum and Workhouse. Both are well worth a visit.

BRUNNER MOND, ICI

Commencing our look at the industrial town of 'Northwich and surrounds', we will begin with the massive conglomerate that became ICI.

In the *History of Cheshire* by J. H. Hanshall, dated 1817, he writes, 'Winnington Hall is described as a large building with nothing particularly striking in its appearance; the situation, however, is delightfully picturesque close to the most romantic part of the River Weaver.'

This description of the area was not to last long, as two businessmen later completely altered this view of Northwich. In 1873, John Brunner and Ludwig Mond formed a partnership and purchased Winnington Hall and its expansive grounds. The hall was built in the late sixteenth or early seventeenth century for a member of the Warburton family of Warburton and Arley in Cheshire. In the early 1800s, a sandstone extension was added to the building.

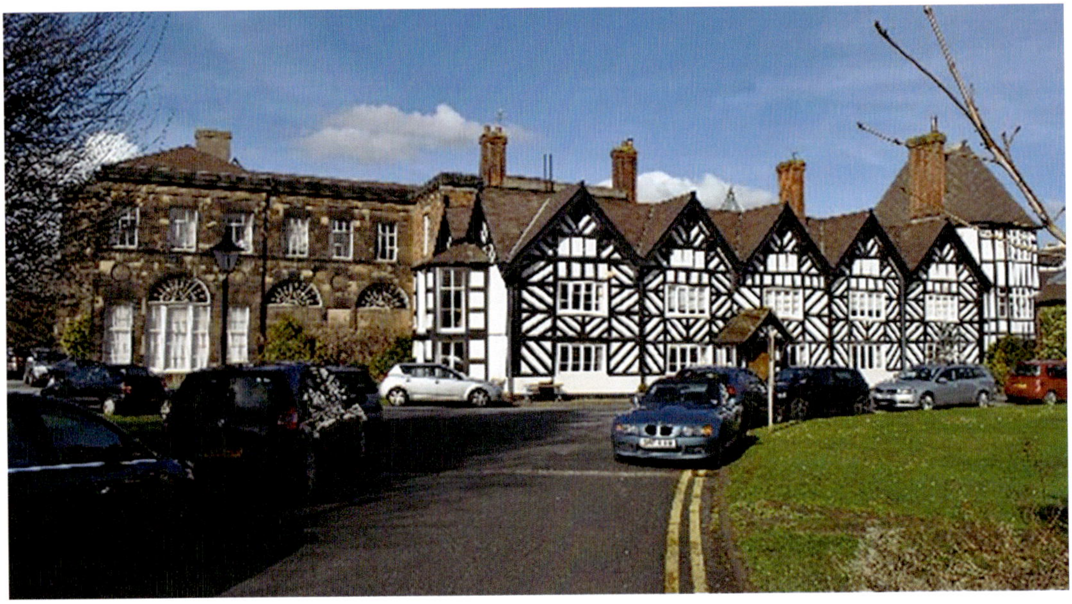

Winnington Hall.

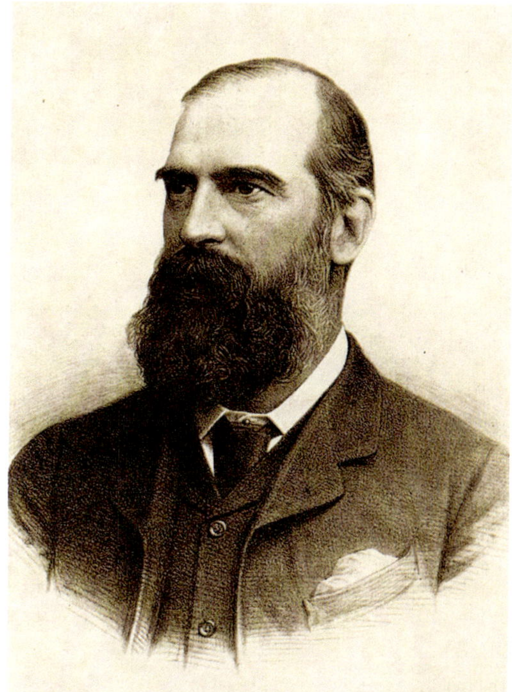

John Brunner and Ludwig Mond.

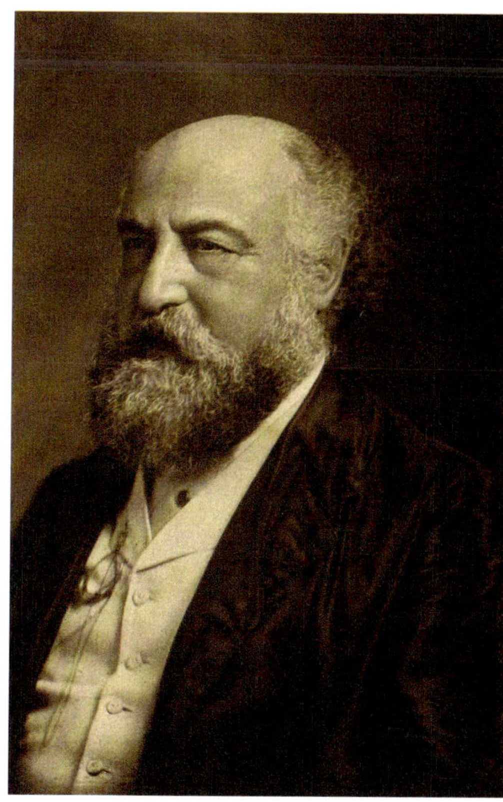

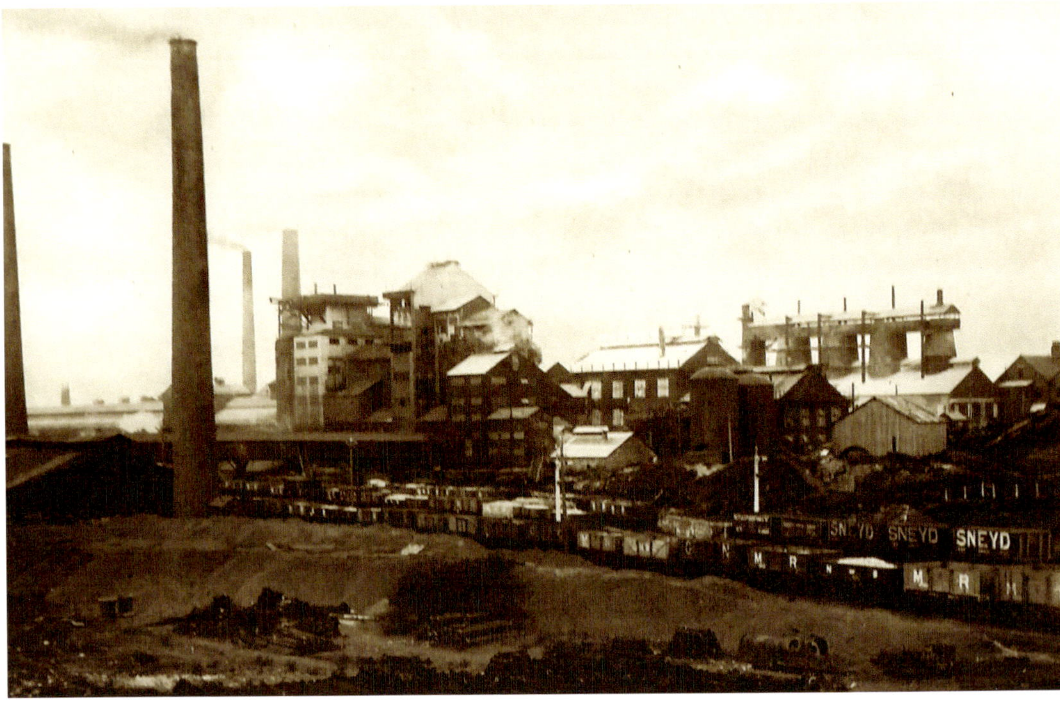

Brunner Mond Company Works, 1923.

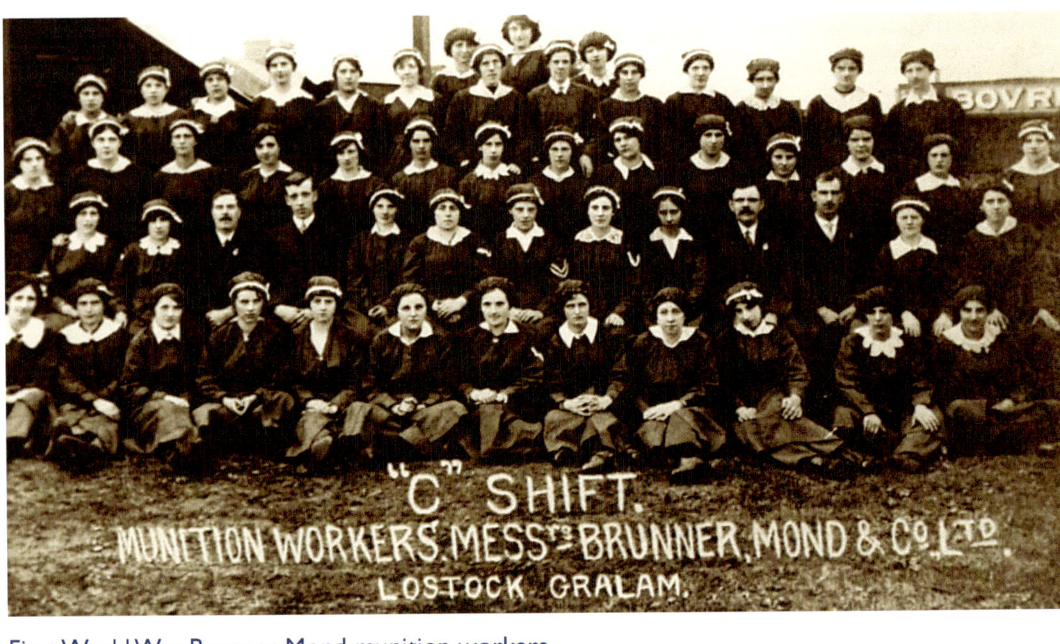

First World War Brunner Mond munition workers.

This beautiful country house later found itself not in the picturesque countryside but in the centre of an industrial complex. John Brunner and Ludwig Mond wanted the estate to build their chemical works, which later became Brunner Mond Ltd, and then ICI (Imperial Chemical Industries). Initially, the plan was to demolish it, but this was later rescinded, and John Brunner and Ludwig Mond moved in with their families. The hall has outlived most of the chemical works that once surrounded it.

However, Brunner and Mond became a limited company, building Winnington Works on the grounds of the hall, and the first batch of soda ash was produced in 1874. Later, Brunner Mond Ltd became one of the world's largest and most successful companies.

Works were built around Cheshire and elsewhere; above is an image of the Winnington Hall. The company went from strength to strength, and over the years, its tentacles spread across Britain and the world. There were ups and downs during this journey, so let us highlight one of the downs.

THE BRUNNER MOND SILVERTOWN DISASTER

A nasty incident occurred in the early days of Brunner Mond after they opened a works in London's docklands to work on soda ash delivered from Winnington Works. In 1894, it began manufacturing soda crystals at its Winnington factory. In 1912, the manufacture of these products ceased, leaving the fully equipped chemical plant idle.

During the First World War, the manufacture of arms and munitions was in significant demand; accordingly, factories were opened across the country. Chemical companies were put to work manufacturing components for shells, bullets and bombs, as well as the means of delivering them.

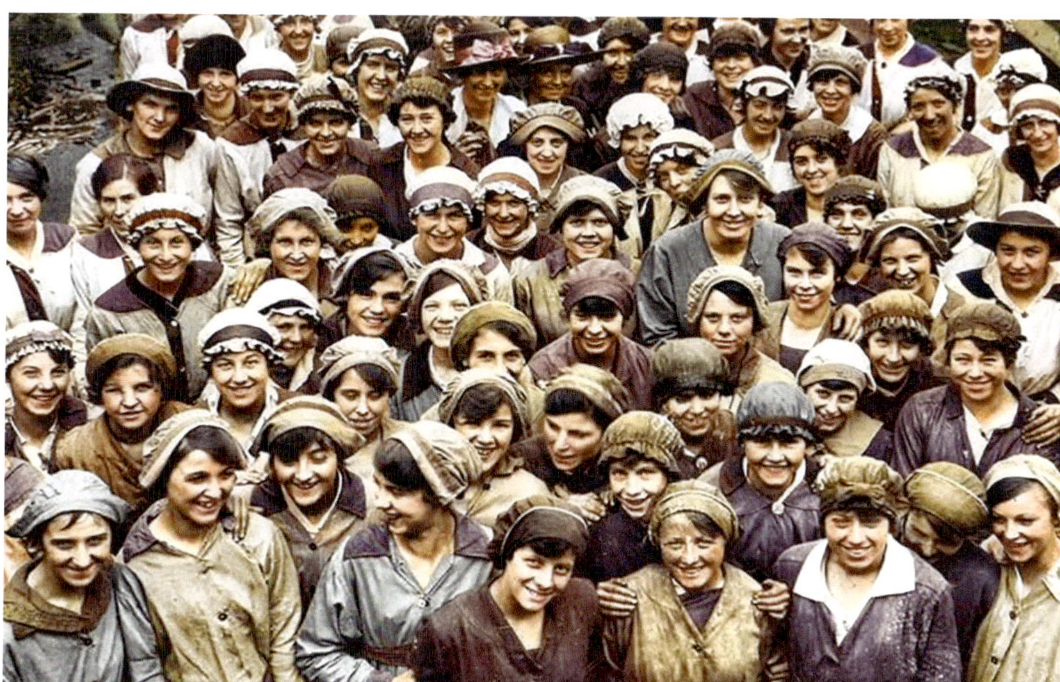

Brunner Mond chemical workers.

In 1914, the First World War began amid a massive munitions shortage, to the point that by 1915 the government was desperately short of shells. They decided to use the redundant Brunner Mond factory in Silvertown to purify TNT for use in munitions. This was even more dangerous than manufacturing the stuff! The method used was invented by Brunner Mond's chief scientist, F.A. Freeth. When the Brunner Mond factory at Silvertown was being planned for conversion to manufacture armaments, the directors of Brunner Mond expressed reservations. Their works were in a densely populated area with 3,000 people living nearby, meaning any accident would have catastrophic consequences. Despite their protestations, the government refused to budge, and the purification of TNT commenced in 1915. The Brunner Mond staff were instructed to treat the highly volatile substance with the greatest care. The plant continued to purify TNT at around 10 tons a day.

All went well for the first fourteen months until 19 January 1917. On this date, a fire broke out, and at 6.50 a.m., efforts were underway to extinguish it when 50 tons of TNT exploded. This destroyed the plant entirely, and the nearby railway wagons were filled with TNT. Houses were damaged and Silvertown Fire Station was destroyed, with debris strewn for miles. Seventy-three people were killed and more than 400 were injured, with damage caused to 70,000 properties in the surrounding area. It was reported that the windows were blown out at the Savoy Hotel on The Strand, and the blast was heard as far away as Norfolk.

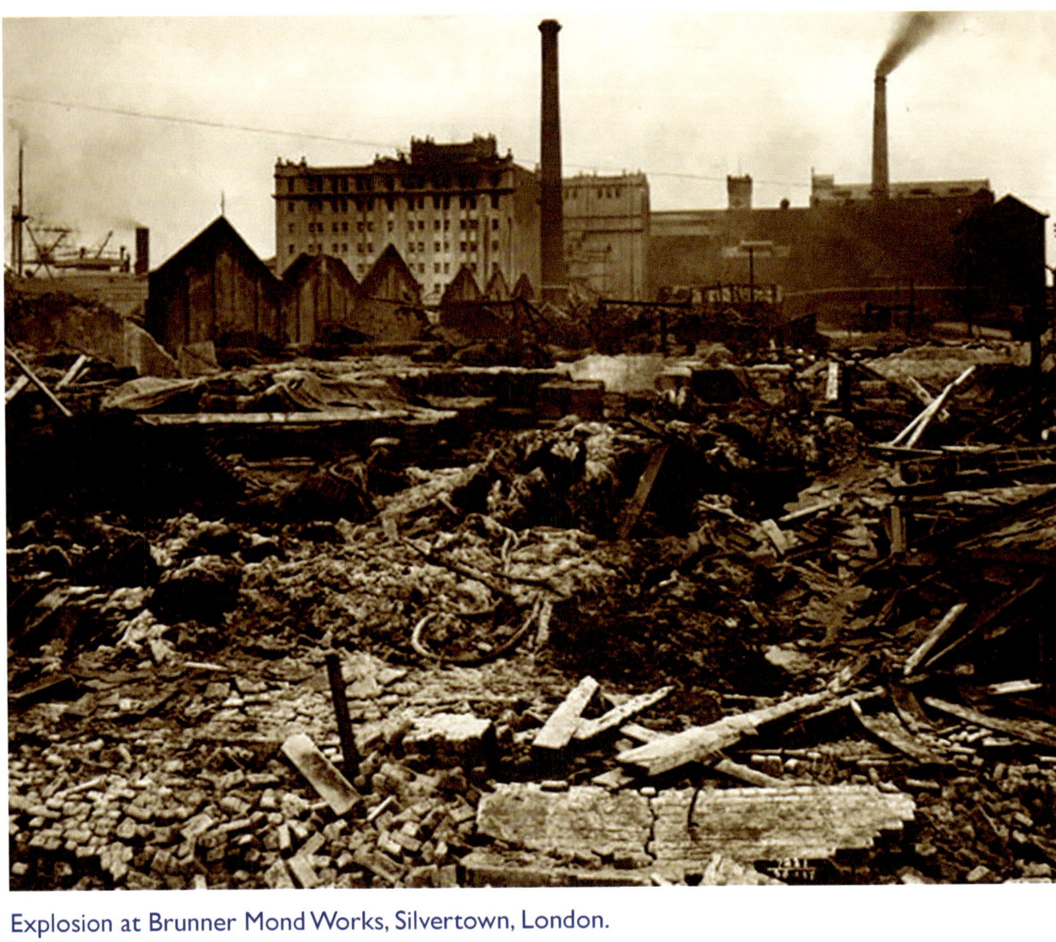

Explosion at Brunner Mond Works, Silvertown, London.

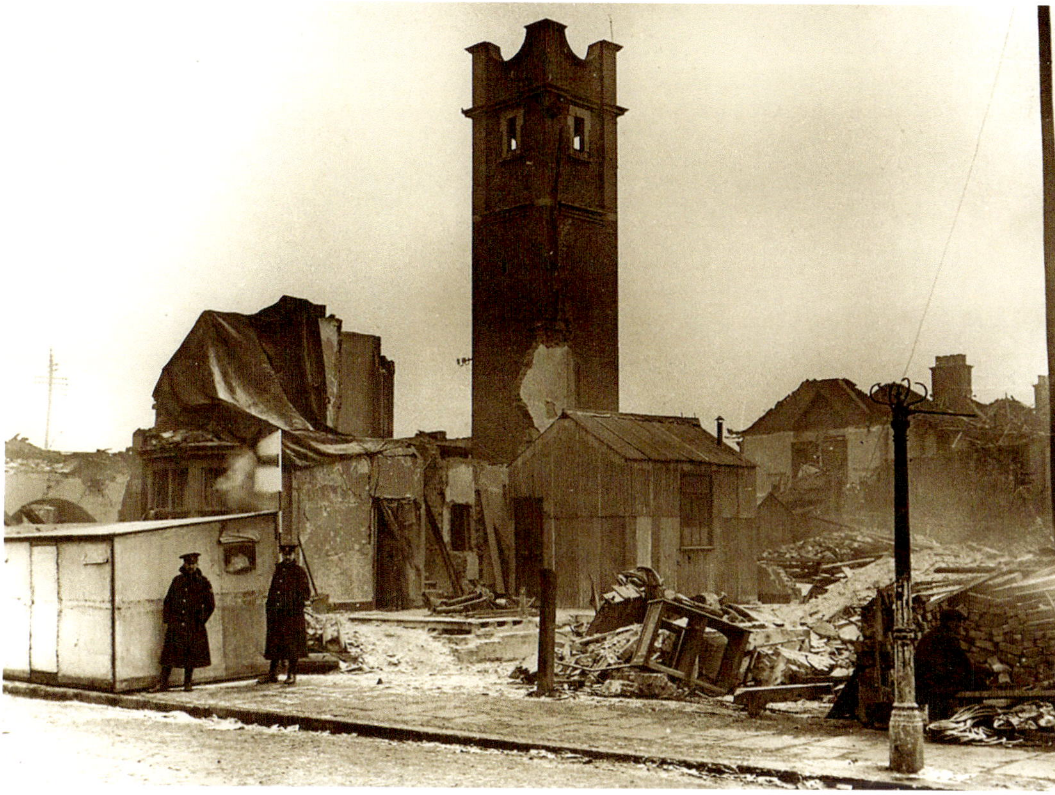

Another photograph of the damage caused.

The plant's relatively low death rate was due to it being Sunday and the factory having only a few staff members present. This explosion is still described as London's biggest to date.

Another factory was built in 1916 to manufacture TNT at an even greater rate than the Silvertown factory. This was situated in Lostock, near Northwich, and was known as the Gadbrook Munitions Factory. After the war, the factory became the well-loved Broadhurst's Bakery, which has now closed. The Silvertown plant was rebuilt after the war and eventually closed in 1961. When it was rebuilt, it became part of the ICI Alkali Division.

TOWARDS THE END OF THE BRUNNER MOND/ICI AND ASSOCIATE OFFSHOOTS

Below we see the managerial staff of Brunner Mond posed in front of the new extension to Winnington Hall.

In December 1926, Brunner Mond became part of Imperial Chemical Industries (ICI). The company was founded with the merger of four companies: Brunner Mond, Nobel Explosives, the United Alkali Company, and British Dyestuffs Corporation.

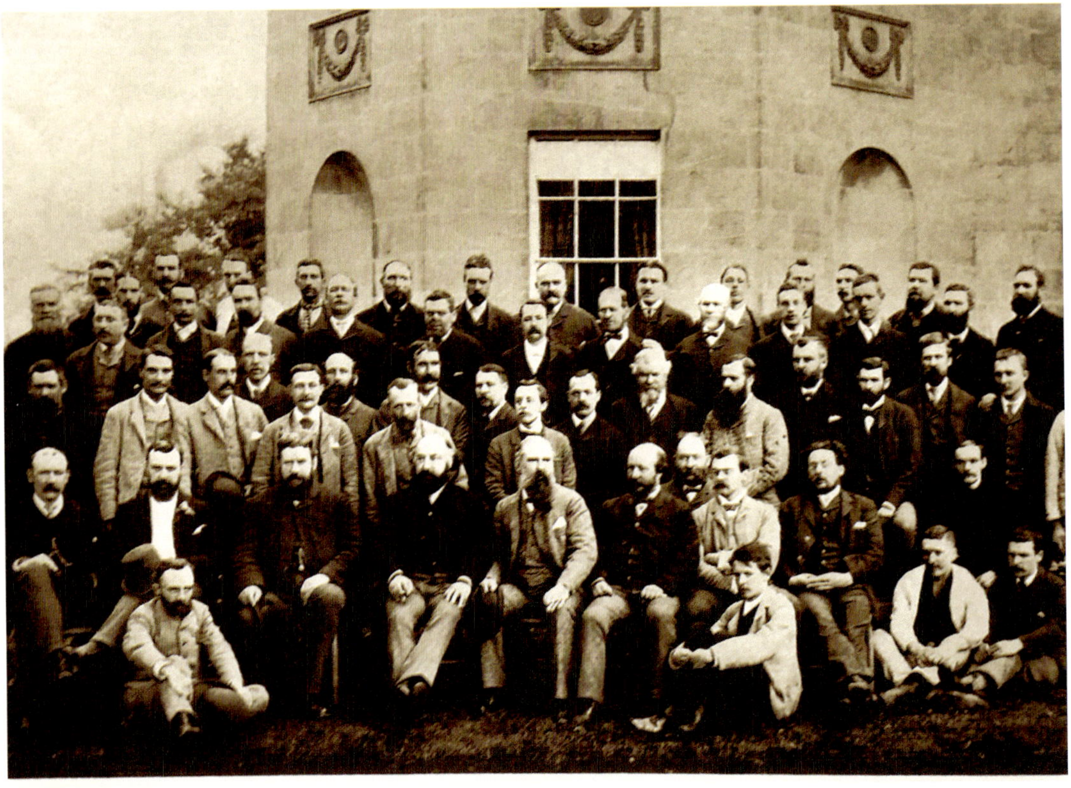

Brunner Mond management staff with new extension to Winnington Hall in the background.

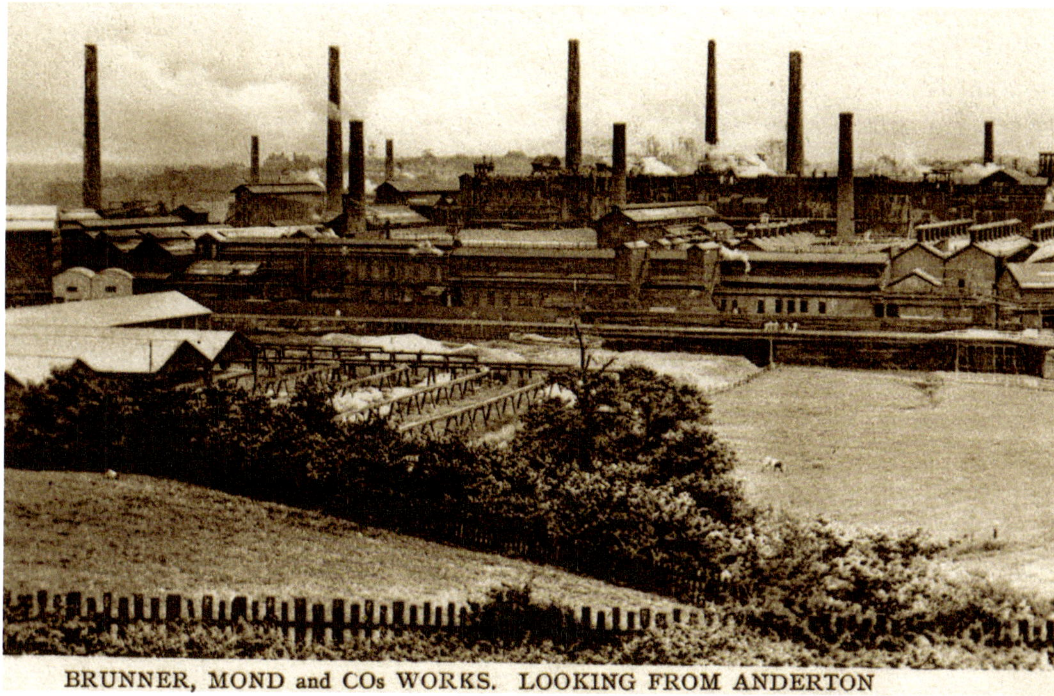

Winnington Works, Northwich.

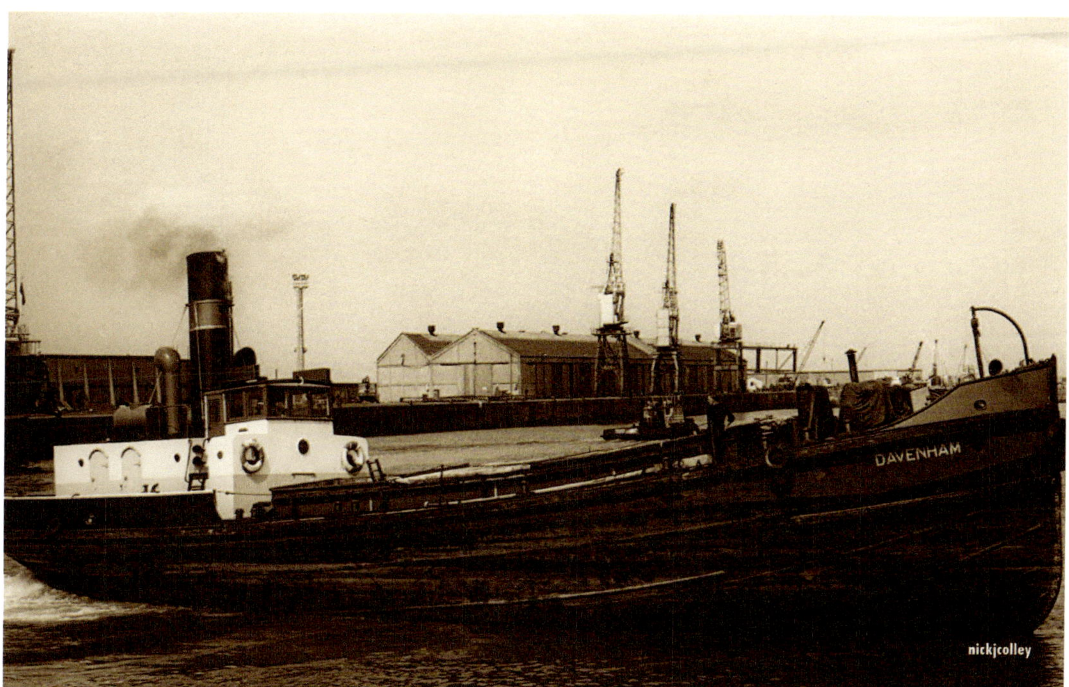

ICI coaster *Davenham*.

It established its head office, Imperial Chemical House at Millbank in London, in 1928. This prestigious building was divided in 1987 to create Norwest House at No. 9 Millbank and Nobel House at No. 17 Smith Square. ICI moved out in 1999.

The companies involved with ICI continued to expand, mainly within the chemical industry, manufacturing products such as fertilisers, dyestuffs and paints. ICI also owned the Sunbeam motorcycle business. It had originally been part of Nobel Industries, which later merged into ICI, and they continued manufacturing motorcycles until 1937. During the Second World War, ICI was engaged with the UK's nuclear weapons programme known as Tube Alloys. After the war, ICI expanded further through numerous acquisitions. By the end of the Second World War, it had become a significant employer in central Cheshire, especially through its Alkali Division. Over the years, and notably after the war extending into the 1950s, they commissioned a fleet of coasters to transport their products to Liverpool Docks. These vessels were given Cheshire village names such as *Anderton*, *Barnton*, *Davenham*, *Weaverham*, *Wincham*, *Cuddington*, *Marbury* and *Marston*, with one exception being *James Jackson Grundy*, named after an ICI manager. Each vessel made two or three trips weekly from Winnington Works on the River Weaver to Liverpool and Birkenhead, transferring chemical products to ocean-going ships. These coasters carried chemicals and soda ash from the ICI works at Northwich down the rivers Weaver and Mersey to Liverpool. The *Davenham* was built by Yarwood's in 1944, and it was commissioned in 1946 for the ICI Alkali Division. It was taken out of service in the 1960s. After a refit, it was sent to the Ellesmere Port Boat Museum, then to the Hebrides, where it was sold to a new owner.

The *Cuddington* was built in 1948 by Yarwood's for the ICI Alkali Division. It worked until the 1970s, then, in 1979, it was displayed at the Boat Museum in Ellesmere Port, where it remains.

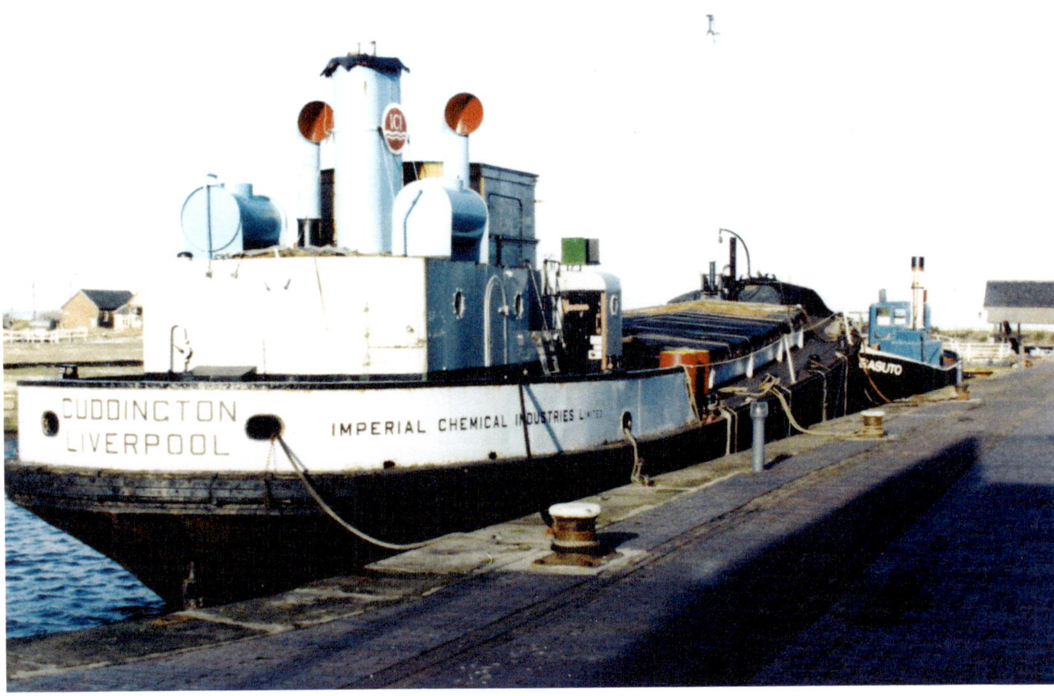

ICI coaster *Cuddington*. (Source: https://shippingandshipbuilding.uk/)

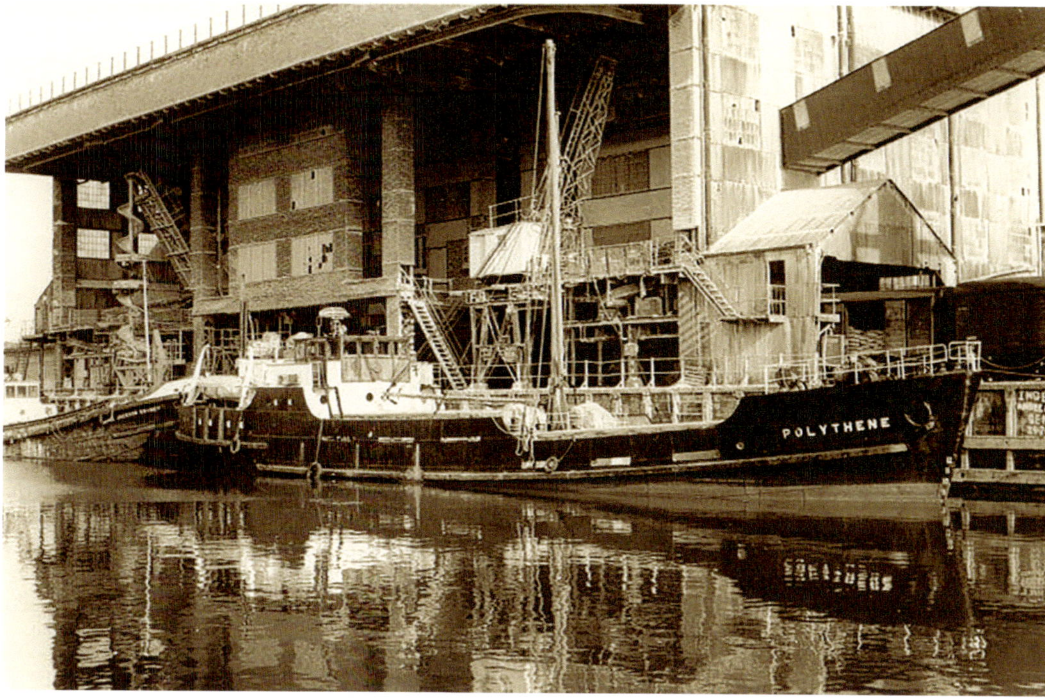

ICI coaster *Polythene*. (Source: *Shipping Today & Yesterday*)

The coaster *Polythene* was not built by Yarwood's this time. A timeline follows.

1949: Completed by Goole Shipbuilding and Repairing Co. Ltd, Goole, in 1949 for ICI Ltd, as *POLYTHENE*.

1972: Sold to A. C. Stewart and W. G. Stewart, Dartford, Kent.

1972: Owners became Stewart Brothers (Shipping) Ltd, Dartford.

1972: Sold to F. A. G. and J. Kennedy, Rochester.

1974: Sold to W. F. Thompson, Ipswich.

1976: Sold to W. S. and A. A. Banks (Pentland Ferries Ltd, managers), St Margaret's Hope, Orkney.

1977: Owners became Hurst Shipping Ltd (Pentland Ferries Ltd, managers), St Margaret's Hope, Orkney.

29 August 1979: Driven ashore and wrecked in Prince Rupert Bay, Dominica. Its anchor chain broke after having been ordered out of harbour to ride out Hurricane David. It had been on a voyage from Roseau to St Vincent with the motor vessel reported to be *Little Stephen* in tow for repairs. It finished its days lying on its side in Trinidad.

Their light railway had grown, and a new link was built from Winnington Works through to Oakleigh Sidings by the Northwich Infirmary. Here, trains carrying limestone, mainly from Buxton, would transfer it from British Railways to the ICI railway. In 1955, ICI owned 142 locomotives, both steam and diesel, and 3,330 main line rail wagons, of which 2,600 were used exclusively within ICI works nationwide. This network had 260 miles of sidings. This gives an example of the size of the ICI company in the country.

The locomotive *Kelvin* was built by E. Burrows & Sons of Sutton, St Helens, in 1908 for Brunner Mond and is seen here at its base at Lostock Works. In the early 1950s, it was still in use at the works and was scrapped at Cox and Danks, Pendleton, in 1955. Note the bell on

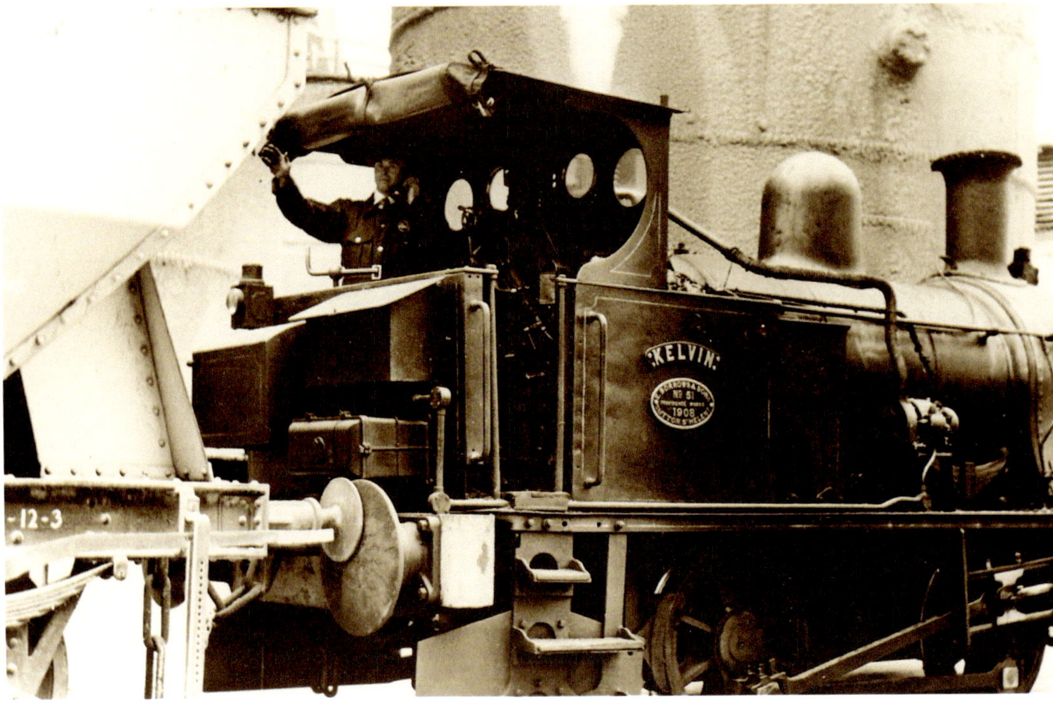

ICI locomotive *Kelvin*.

the side. Before the introduction of two-way radios, all ICI locomotives had a bell that was operated by the drive gear to warn of their approach. Until the introduction of radios, each locomotive required a team of four men. After that, it was reduced to two: a driver and a mate.

Prefab houses were built on Winnington Avenue, Northwich, for Brunner Mond employees. These homes were intended to have a short lifespan due to the council estates to be built to replace them. However, they were warm and comfortable, and so were used for a longer period than intended. Council estates were built in the late forties and early fifties, mainly to house families made homeless during the war and ICI workers coming in from the cities.

Houses were provided for the senior managers, and below we look at one called Lea House in Winnington. It had been known by different names and, over the years, had other uses, but remained in place until the 1950s. Lea House is shown on an 1882 map across from a house called Shell Cottage on Winnington Road, and just fifteen years later, the name had changed to The Ley. It was a seven-bedroom mansion with a coach house, stables and an extensive garden. Records show that a solicitor occupied it, William Sutton Bradburne, who was documented in the 1874 County Directory & Gazetteer as living at The Lay (another name for the same house). Following Bradburne's death in 1886, the house was put up for auction. By 1891 it was thought to have been purchased by Brunner Mond and occupied by Thomas Forgan from Scotland, a senior manager at the company, living there with his wife and a family of eight daughters. The house remained a part of the Brunner Mond site into the twentieth century and was used as a Red Cross auxiliary hospital during the First World War. It was under the management of Lady Charlotte Jarmay, the wife of the Brunner Mond managing director Gustav Jarmay (later known as Sir John Jarmay). Gustav was born in Budapest, Hungary, in 1856. He studied sciences in Zurich and London and gained his Certificate of Naturalisation

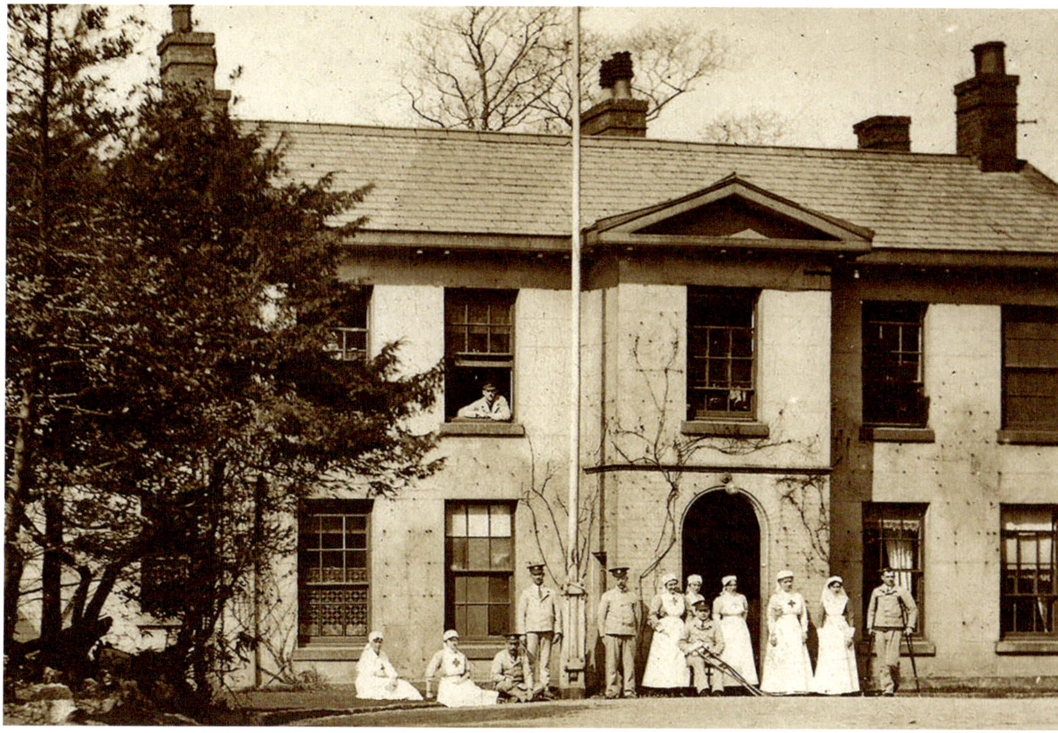

'The Ley' as a Red Cross hospital during the First World War.

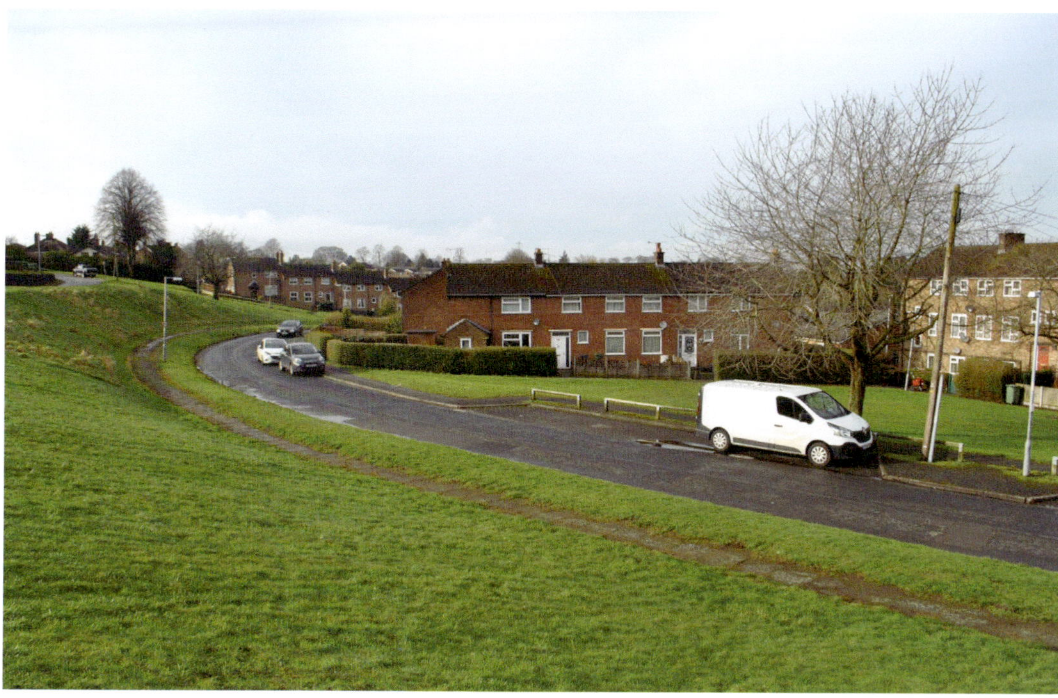

Weaverham council houses mainly allocated to ICI workers.

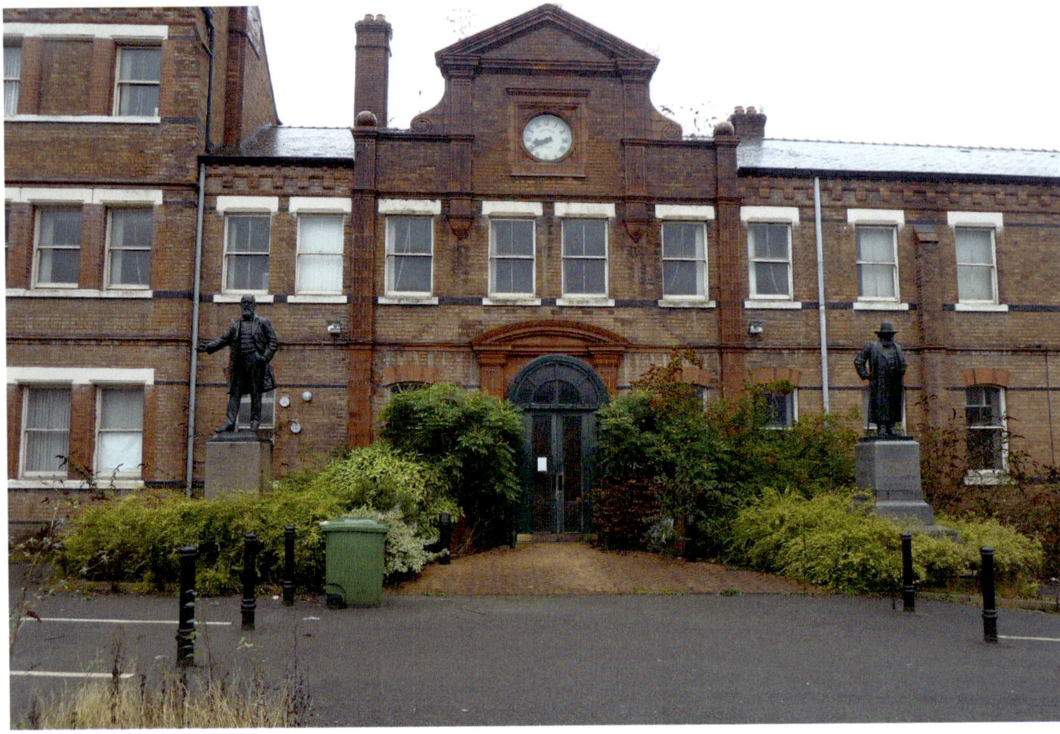

Mond House.

in 1914. He was knighted for his services to the war effort, as recommended by the Ministry of Munitions, specifically for his work on the high explosives he had invented. Lady Charlotte was the officer in charge of the Ley Hospital and was awarded an OBE for her work there during the war.

The Jarmays also lived in Hartford Lodge, more commonly known now as Whitehall on School Lane, Hartford. John Douglas Senior, father of the more famous architect John Douglas from Cuddington, was also an architect and builder. He was responsible for, among other properties, Hartford Lodge. Note the similarity in the front elevation of both houses, probably copied from the Ley, which was built before his time.

Sir John Jarmay was a well-known member of the Cheshire hunting set. It was reported that in 1914, a hundred Belgian refugees were brought to Northwich and accommodated at the Bachelor's Hall, Winnington, whilst a further seventeen would be provided for in the Ley, both at the expense of Brunner Mond. During the 1920s, the Ley was used as a private school; the headmistress was Mrs Ellen Keating of Cassia Lodge, Whitegate. Throughout the 1930s and 1940s, various events were held at the Ley, as advertised in the local newspapers, including first aid lectures and Anglo-Polish community meetings. In 1954, the Claudia Stansfield School of Dancing also held regular classes at this location.

In the mid-1950s, the Ley was demolished to make way for the new Brunner House building. Brunner House was a multistorey office block occupied by the ICI, and many Northwich folk will have vivid memories of it during the 1960s–80s. At its height, it housed over 1,000 ICI employees. The site was given the go-ahead for demolition in 1997 and was replaced by a large private housing estate in the early 2000s.

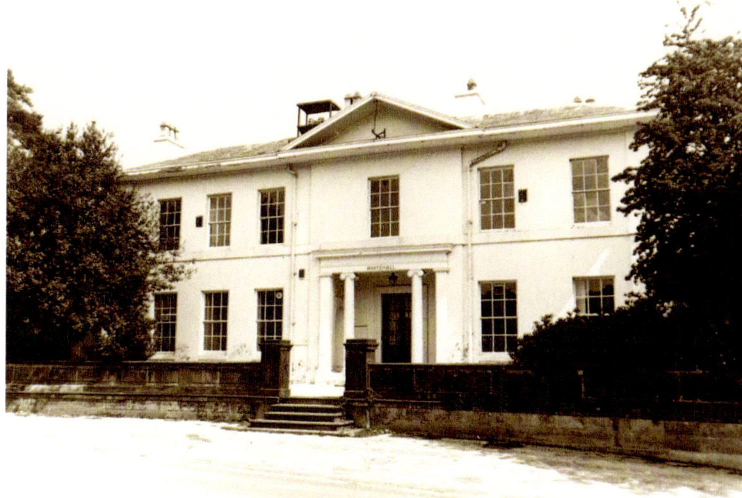

'Whitehall', also known as Hartford Lodge.

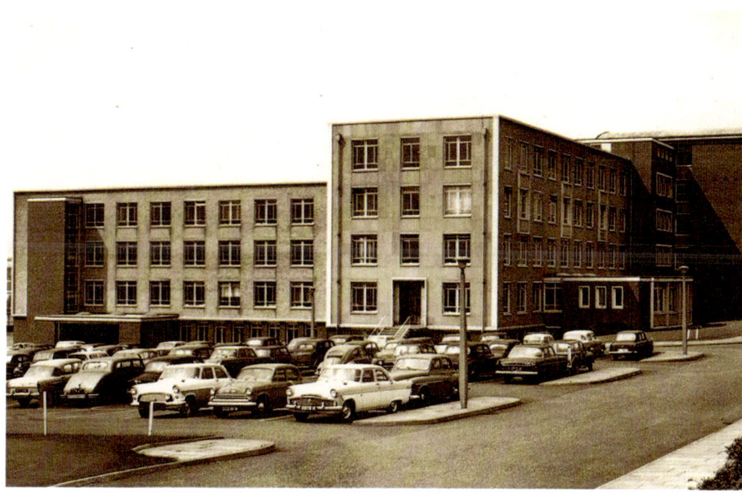

Brunner House ICI offices.

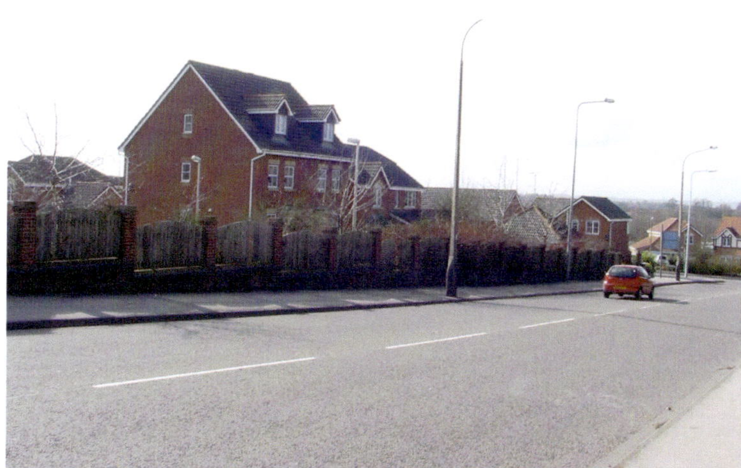

Location of demolished Brunner House.

THE DISCOVERY OF POLYTHENE

Perhaps one of the common complaints today is the amount of plastic that blights the beaches and public places. It harms sea creatures and birds, and blocks drains. Supermarkets love it. Environmentalists and the green lobby hate it. But almost everyone uses it. Polythene is the world's most widely used plastic and was used to make billions of carrier bags each year, as well as nearly everything else that involves plastic and its derivatives. Yet it was first discovered, by accident, at the ICI Wallerscote Works near Northwich. It is only fair to mention that a German scientist in 1900 had the same results but disregarded them.

Now, the story of polythene – and its role in saving thousands of lives in the Second World War, as a more successful method of sealing undersea cables, and in many other essential uses – originated in Northwich.

Polyethylene is also known as synthetic polythene, and it was first produced in 1933 by two researchers, Eric Fawcett and Reginald Gibson, at the ICI laboratories, Wallerscote Works. They were experimenting with a method to make synthetic rubber and stumbled upon polyethylene while working with ethylene. What they had discovered was a white, waxy substance which would change the world, not always for the better. .

Here is an image of a pillbox made from the first batch of polythene, presented to Frank Bebbington in 1936. Frank Bebbington was a research scientist at Wallerscote works and was involved in the discovery of polythene. He worked with Leslie Seed and Cliff Salt, as well as Reginald Gibson and Eric Fawcett, during the research stage and the discovery of polythene.

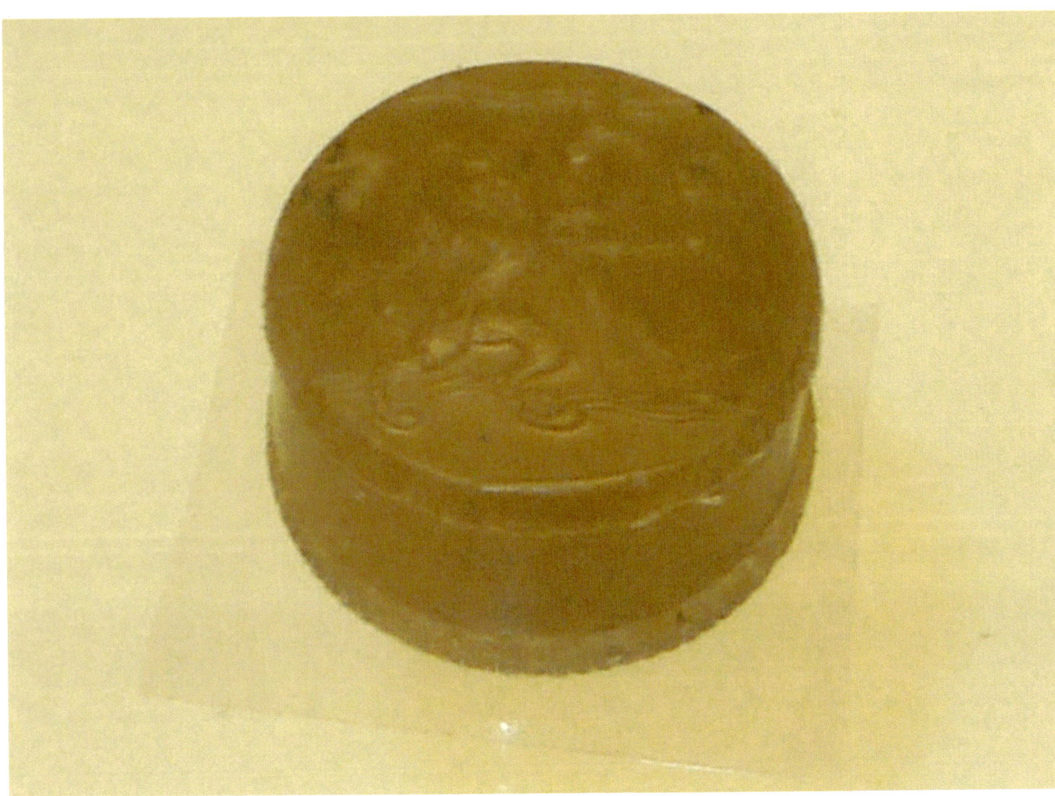

A polythene pillbox. (Credit: Geni)

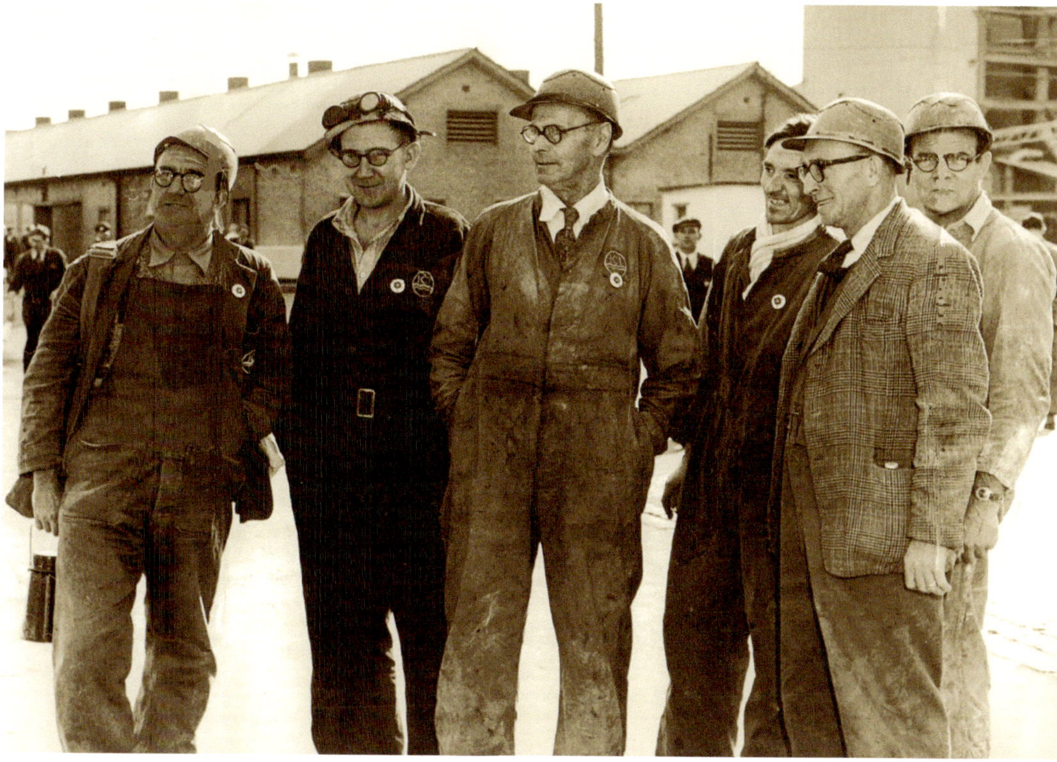

ICI Wallerscote workmen.

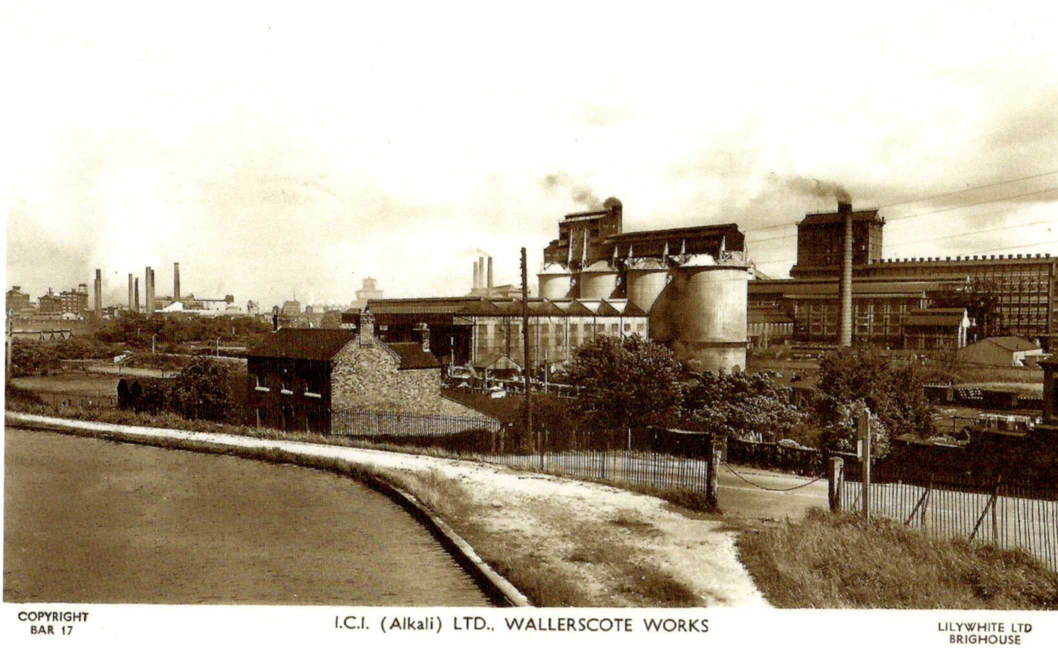

Another look at Wallerscote Works.

The discovery was announced in 1935, and ICI began commercial production of polyethene in 1939. Plastics are now everywhere. From toys to the shopping bags used for groceries (now being replaced by paper), and from food packaging to protective layers for wires, plastics are a part of our everyday electronics and numerous other applications, making them all-pervasive. Polyethylene, more popularly known as polythene, was one of the first plastics that came into widespread use. ICI built the first production plant, which came online during the Second World War.

In the 1950s, living near the plant, one became accustomed to frequent explosions and finding bits of what is now known as raw polythene in the area. The reason was that unless the plant was shut down for two weeks every two or three years, it would explode. ICI initially decided to halt production on this basis, but after a year, the warning came too late, and the plant blew up. It was rebuilt using prefabricated units, which ICI found to be cheaper than losing two weeks of production. From then on, the plant was allowed to explode and was then rebuilt around the concrete skeleton. An explosion-proof plant was not built until 1978. ICI went onwards and upwards as a major company with many factories worldwide, manufacturing an eclectic mix of products.

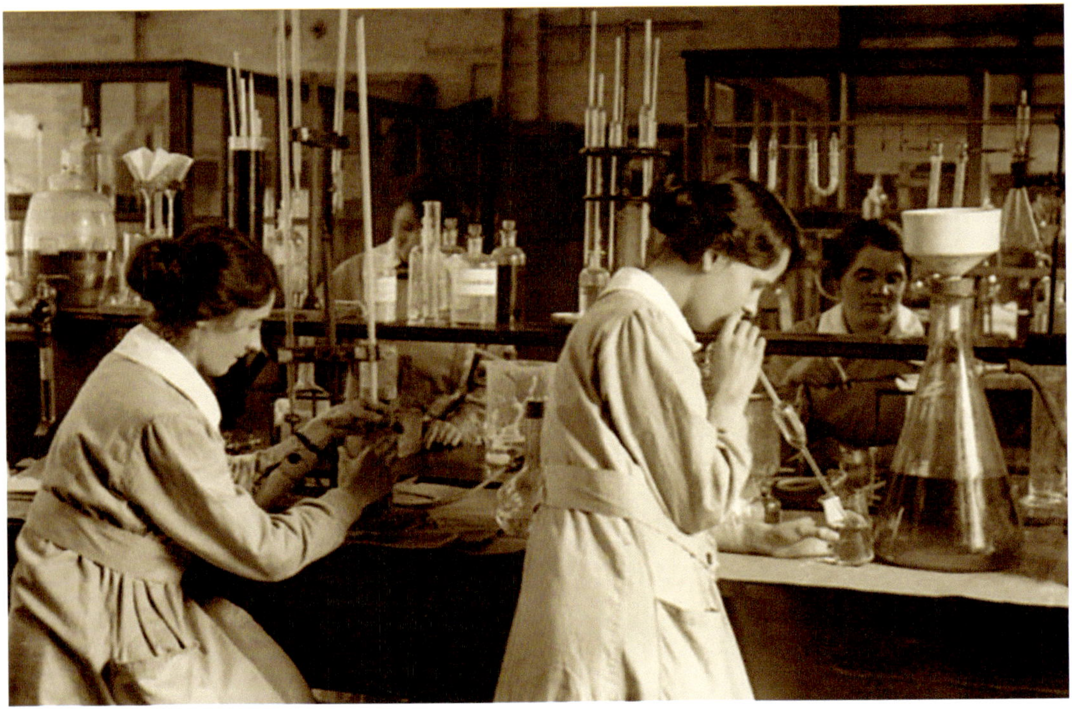

Scientific work in the Wallerscote laboratories.

REDISCOVERY OF SALT IN CHESHIRE AND MARBURY HALL

The Domesday Book provides the earliest written record of salt making in Northwich, mentioning a salt house belonging to Earl Hugh Lupus. The salt beds of Northwich were rediscovered in 1670 by employees of the local Merbury family of Marbury Hall. The family was looking for coal when they accidentally discovered rock salt in the grounds. It was John Jackson of Halton who discovered the salt while looking for coal on the instructions of William Merbury, the owner of Marbury Hall. This led to the Northwich salt businesses and, through them, to the spectacular subsidence that later occurred in and around Northwich. Natural brine had been taken from the ground since the very early days of the Romans, and the few deposits of rock salt that were discovered had simply been used as cattle licks. After this, rock salt mining took priority.

One of the reasons John Brunner and Ludwig Mond decided to set up their chemical company in Mid Cheshire was that there were ample supplies of salt for their soda ash production. Many of the products made by ICI and its subsidiaries continued to grow in strength. The products were exported worldwide, and the company expanded with new projects and infrastructure.

Marbury is a small village in Mid Cheshire, not to be confused with Marbury in Cheshire East, nearer to Whitchurch. The Mid Cheshire village in 1260 was a burh, which was part of an Anglo-Saxon fortified manor. The name Marbury means 'the burh by a lake'. There are many lakes or meres around the village; not all were formed by salt mining this time, but ice age glacial depressions filled with water.

In 1865, Marbury consisted of seventeen inhabitants. In the reign of King Henry III, the manor of Marbury was held by the ancient family of Merbury or Marbury, who resided in Marbury Hall. On the death of Richard Marbury in 1684, the family name became extinct. In 1708, the hall was purchased by Richard, Earl Rivers of Rock Savage. It was passed to his daughter on her marriage to James, Earl of Barrymore, and then to the earl's second son, the Hon. Richard Barry, then to his son, the Hon. John Barry.

Here we look at an old Mid Cheshire hall that stood until it was demolished, like many of its kind.

The hall in 1865 was described as a spacious brick mansion that had recently undergone extensive renovations; in fact, it had been virtually rebuilt. The renowned architectural historian Nicolas Pevsner compared the remodelled hall with Wellington College and

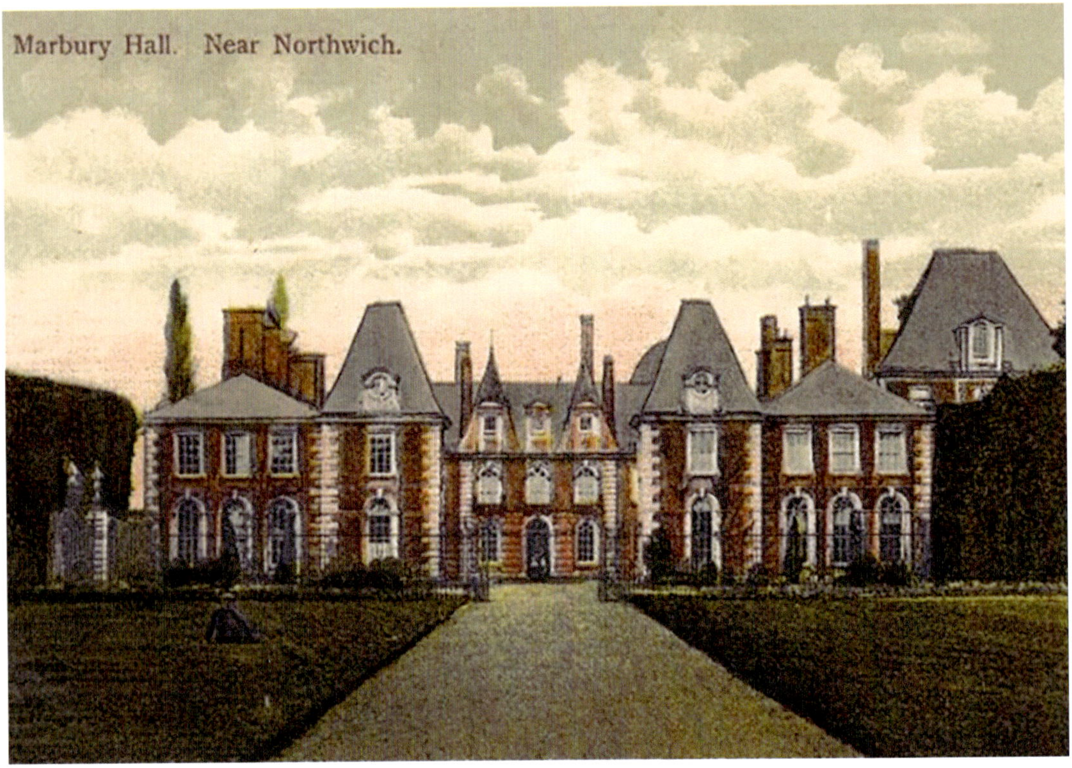

Marbury Hall.

described it as 'quite a document of architectural history'. Then, during the Second World War, British soldiers camped in the grounds, and roads were built for the military. Amongst other servicemen, survivors of Dunkirk were billeted there.

After the war, the hall was sold to ICI to house their workers. The men of the family lived there until they were allocated a council house, or one of the refurbished army huts. My father was one such man who left the family in Liverpool and lived at the hall until a house in Farm Road, Weaverham, was allocated for the family.

In January 1969, the hall was demolished against the wishes of locals and historians alike. Nicolas Pevsner called it a 'great pity'.

James Barry, 4th Earl of Barrymore, the earl's son-in-law, became the owner. He enlarged the house, and it then passed to the earl's younger son, Richard Barry. Richard died in 1787, and the house passed to James Hugh Smith Barry, who also owned adjacent Belmont Hall, now Cransley School.

Many important artworks, including masterpieces and Roman and Greek sculptures, were housed in Belmont Hall and moved to Marbury Hall when the Smith-Barrys sold Belmont Hall in 1801, after James Hugh Smith Barry died. He had requested in his will that Marbury Hall be extended to house the artworks.

It was not until the 1850s that the hall was eventually enlarged and remodelled by architect Anthony Salvin, based on the French chateau of Fontainebleau. The gardens and an 80-acre lake were designed by landscape gardener John Nesfield, who was also instrumental in planting the famous Lime Avenue of trees, which remains today.

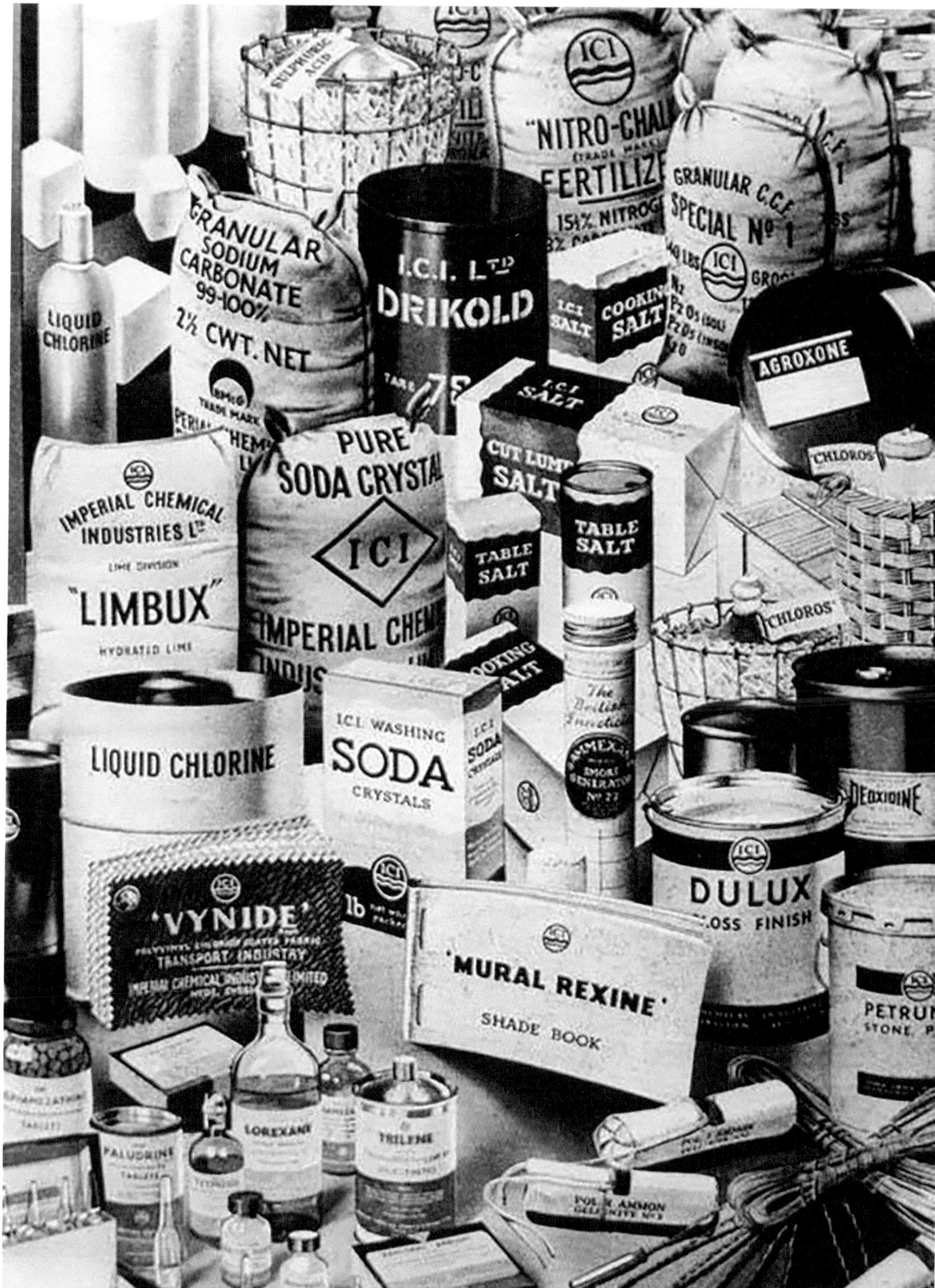

ICI products.

The house stayed in the Smith-Barry family until 1932, when it was sold and became a country club. The artwork was sold and dispersed, including pieces of the Parthenon Frieze, dating back to c. 445 BC and forming part of the Elgin Marbles, that are now in the British Museum. Another artefact, an ancient Roman statue of Zeus, is housed in the Getty Museum in America.

There are many legends associated with Marbury Hall, including the following two. In the 1700s, a horse is said to have raced from London to Marbury for a large bet, and when it arrived, it drank from the mere and died. The horse (an equine hero of the day) was buried by the side of the mere and is remembered by the following rhyme passed down through the years:

This horse was bred from Marbury Dun
The finest mare that ever run
Run fourteen miles in fifteen hours
And never sweat a hair
Come from London to Marbury from sunrise to sunset for a wager
And when she died, they buried her with silver shoes upon her feet
And wrapped her in a linen sheet.

The White Lady of Marbury is the second legend. There are many versions of the story; briefly, they share a similar theme: that James Hugh Smith Barry (1748–1801) travelled extensively, amassed his art collection, and met an Egyptian girl during his journey. Apparently, she followed him home and lived with him. She asked that if she died before him, that he would embalm and

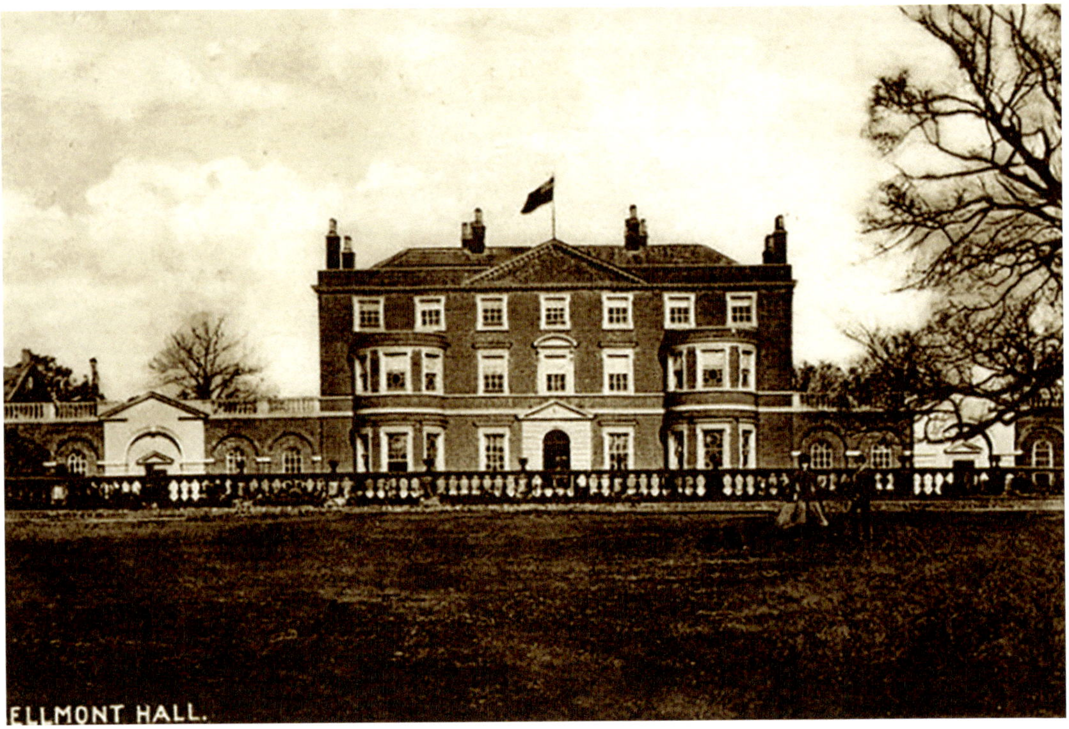

Belmont Hall.

keep her body in a chest beneath the stairs. He did this, but when he died, the family removed the body to Great Budworth churchyard, which is when the hauntings began.

In 1940, the hall was commandeered for use as a military camp during the Second World War. Roads and huts were built, and they housed survivors of the Dunkirk evacuation. Marbury Hall became known as Camp 180, a prisoner-of-war camp, and one famous occupant at that time was Bert Trautmann, a German paratrooper who later became the goalkeeper for Manchester City Football Club. He famously continued playing in a match after breaking his neck.

After the war in 1948, the hall/land was sold to ICI and initially served as its Polish workers' home. However, the huts were subsequently converted into temporary dwellings for those waiting on council lists. The hall once more became a social club, and ICI maintained a swimming pool for its employees. ICI put the hall up for sale in 1961, although it retained the swimming pool. The hall and land immediately surrounding it were sold to a property development company from Manchester, Leslie Fink. The house sadly deteriorated over the years, and in 1968 the hall was demolished.

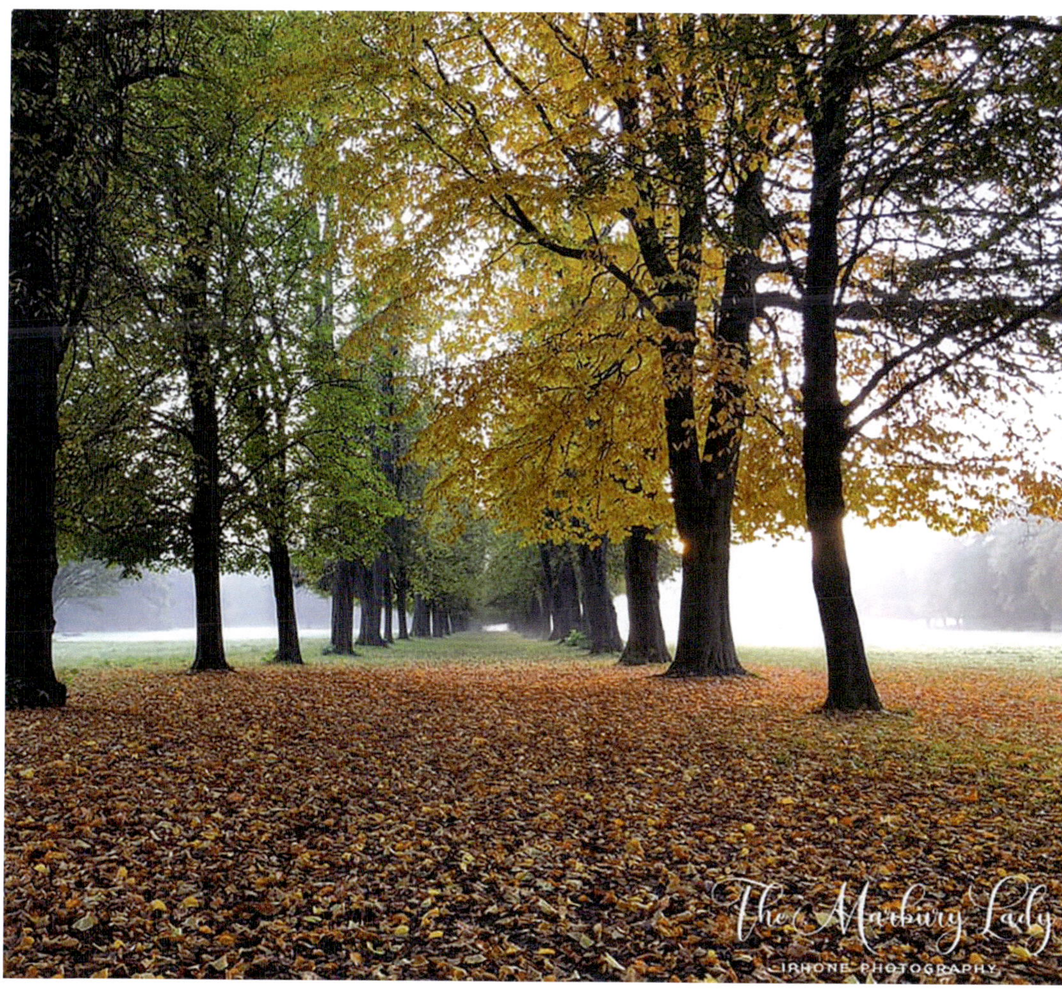

Marbury's Lime Avenue of trees. (Credit: Alison Hamlin Hughes)

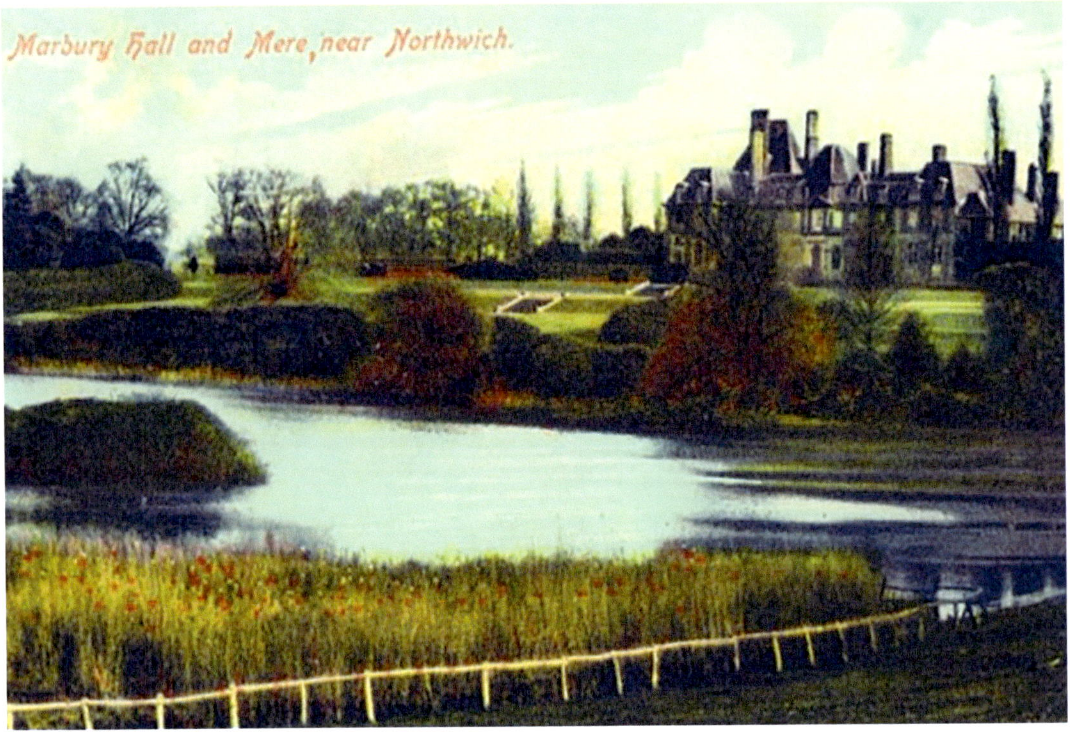

Marbury Hall and Mere.

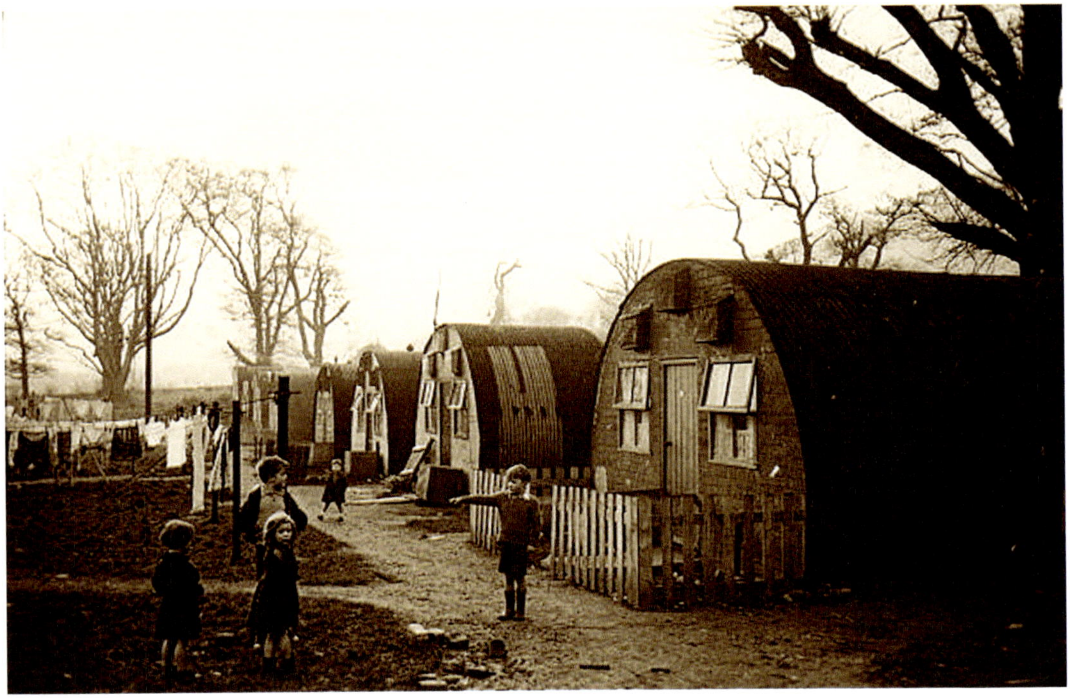

Marbury Hall army huts.

MINING SALT AND EXTRACTING BRINE

The salt beds of Cheshire were formed 200 million years ago during the Triassic period. Seawater moved inland from an open sea, creating a chain of shallow salt marshes across what is today the Cheshire Basin. As the marshes evaporated, deep deposits of rock salt were formed. It was extracted as brine, and using pans on the surface, it was boiled to produce granules of white salt. There is evidence of this process in the Roman period. From the seventeenth century, it was mined as rock salt, initially for cattle licks.

Rock salt could be mined by drilling with mechanical tools into the salt and transporting it to the surface. The other method, and the one that caused the most damage, is brine pumping, in which water is pumped into the rock salt, then drawn up to the surface and into vast receptacles heated from below, as photographed within this book. As the water evaporates, the salt is left dry; it is then bagged and stacked, ready for distribution.

Herein lies the problem: the huge chasms are left underground to collapse, causing surface damage. This no longer applies when mining rock salt at Winsford.

Salt mining took off in a big way, and the successful salt barons became fabulously wealthy. But this had its problems. When underground chasms are created after removing the salt, they can collapse, bringing down everything above them, including buildings. This is a very old image of salt mining, done by hand with a pick and shovel, which was perhaps easier than coal mining, as the salt crystals are, in the main, quite soft to deal with.

In the image overleaf we see the trucks that salt was transported in, pulled by pit ponies.

Northwich suffered the most, with some damage in nearby Winsford, but the damage in Northwich would be spectacular.

Let's look at what else could be developed using the massive underground caverns. Poland has utilised a salt cavern to construct an underground cathedral and a dance hall, both open to the public. There are a few photographs of such underground features in Cheshire, but here is one from Poland, similar to the one mentioned next.

The Wieliczka Salt Mine, near Kraków, reaches a maximum depth of 327 metres (1,073 feet). This historic mine extends over 245 kilometres (153 miles) and has nine levels (source: The Wieliczka Salt Mine).

The *Illustrated London News*, in the issue dated 24 August 1850, published an article on the salt mines of Northwich, focusing mainly on the Marston salt mine.

At one time, as early as 1850, salt was burdened with a heavy duty of £30 a ton, or £4,488.77 in today's money. However, the duty had been abolished as of 1842, making salt far more

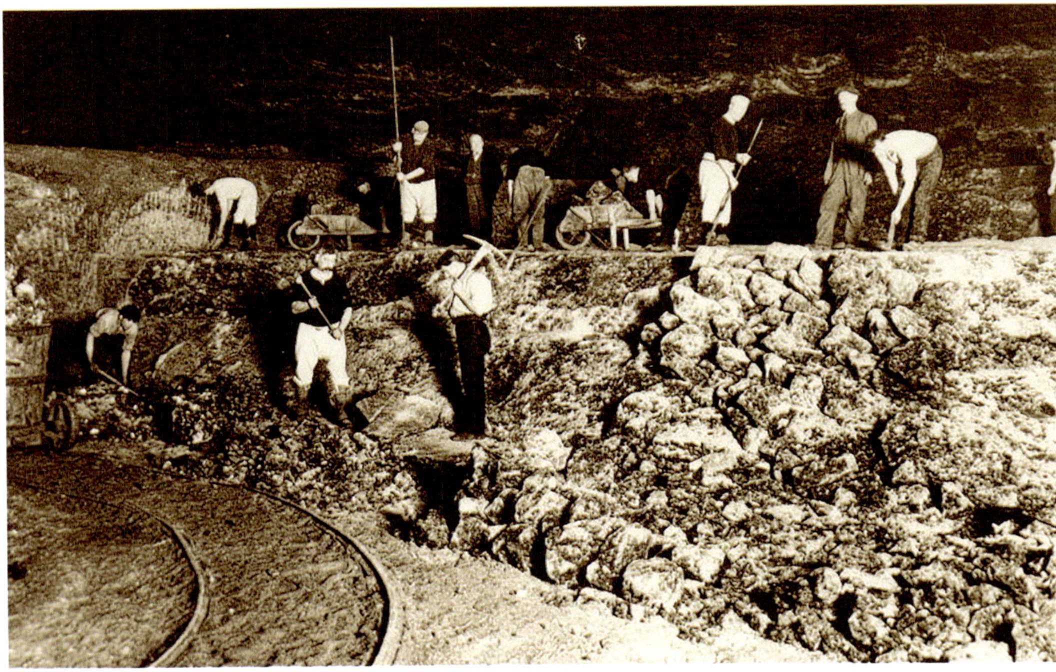

Old Northwich salt mine.

affordable. After the abolition of the tax duty, the wholesale price fell to 6*s* 6*d* per ton, or £35.50 in today's money.

The Adelaide Mine at Marston, owned by Joseph Verdin's company, made a profit not only from salt but also from being a tourist attraction. Local people were allowed to view the spectacle, and Grand Duke Michael of Russia visited. The mine covered 35 acres and formed a vast cavern, like the Winsford salt mine does today.

This allowed as many as 900 people to dance the night away, albeit it took a while to get them all down there. In 1844, it was illuminated by over 10,000 candles during a banquet for Grand Duke Michael of Russia and the Royal Society of England. This huge banqueting hall sparkled in orange light from the walls, floors and ceiling and the many twinkling candle lights – all 130 feet below the surface of Marston. The mine was situated below what is now the lake in Ollershaw Lane. In 1928, this underground spectacular and working mine, like many Northwich mines, suffered flooding. The only casualties were three pit ponies, and the mine eventually collapsed in upon itself, leaving the lake to appear above.

As mentioned earlier, here we have an example of a brine reduction plant. In this image of an old salt works, the man at the bottom is the stoker who kept the fires burning to heat the large tray above, where the white salt would be boiled and removed from the pan to be packed into tubs when evaporation was complete. The clinker from the many works in Winsford was used to build buildings, including houses for the salt workers, including the old Meadow Bank school. The name that it went by in those days was basse.

In the packing room, the dried salt would be bagged, ready for distribution.

The last operational mine was The Lion Saltworks in Ollershaw Lane, Marston, close to the defunct Adelaide mine and the lake that it caused. The Lion Saltworks remained active into the 1980s, when it closed, and was subsequently preserved as a visitor centre and museum. The office inside was once a pub for the workers – dealing with salt was a very thirsty occupation.

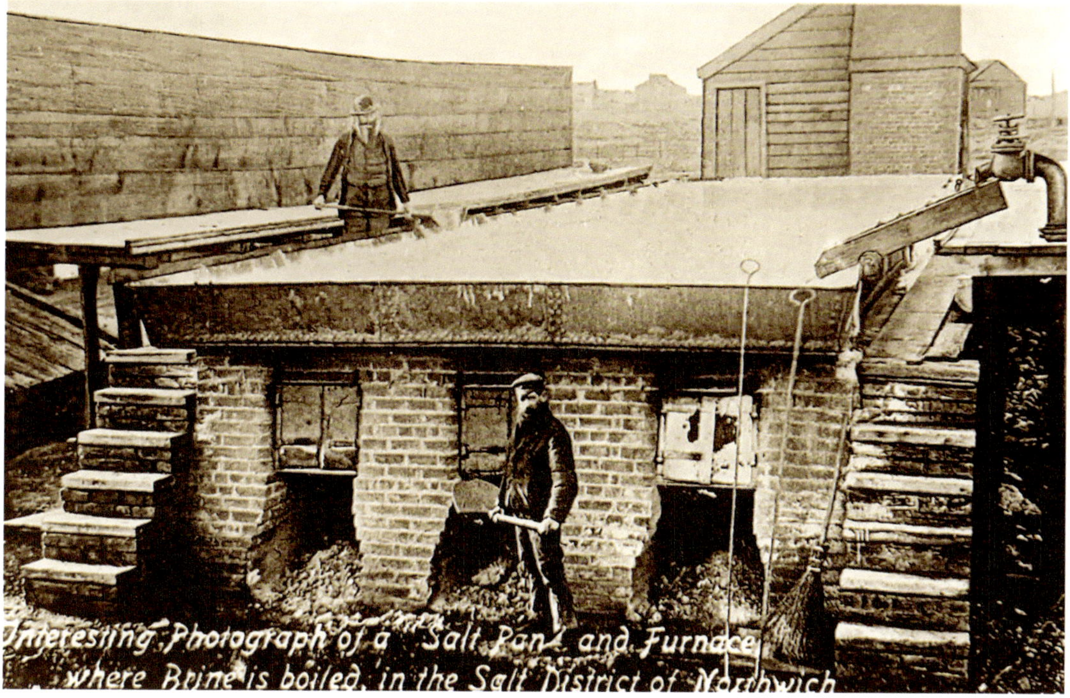

Northwich salt works.

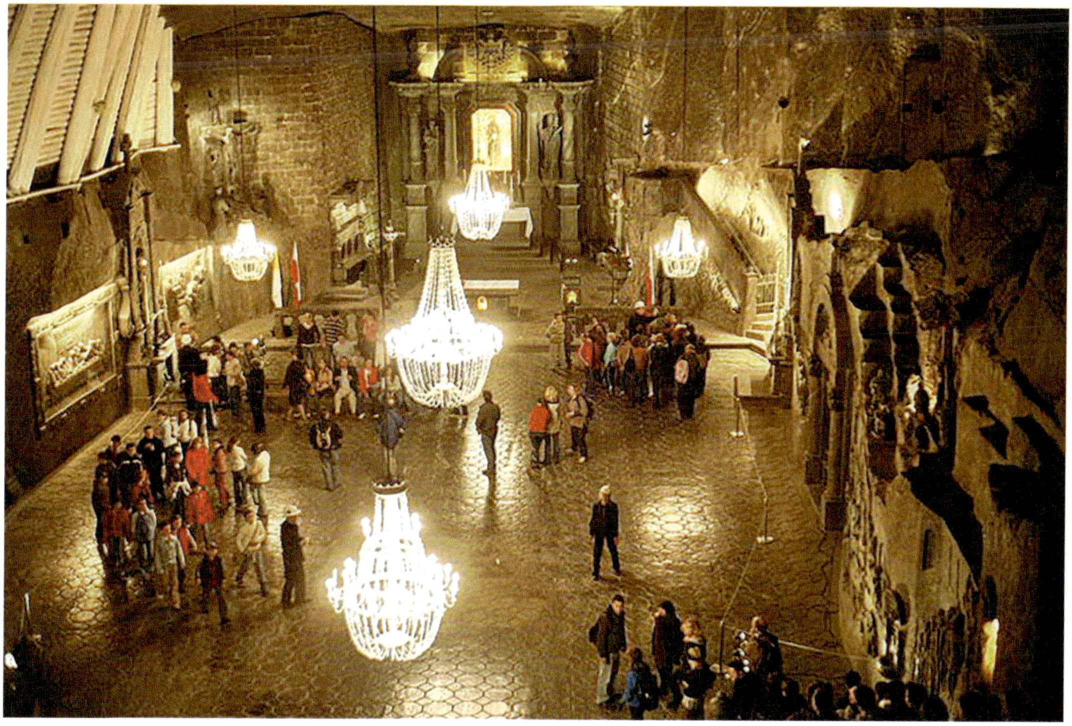

Wieliczka Salt Mine with an underground cathedral.

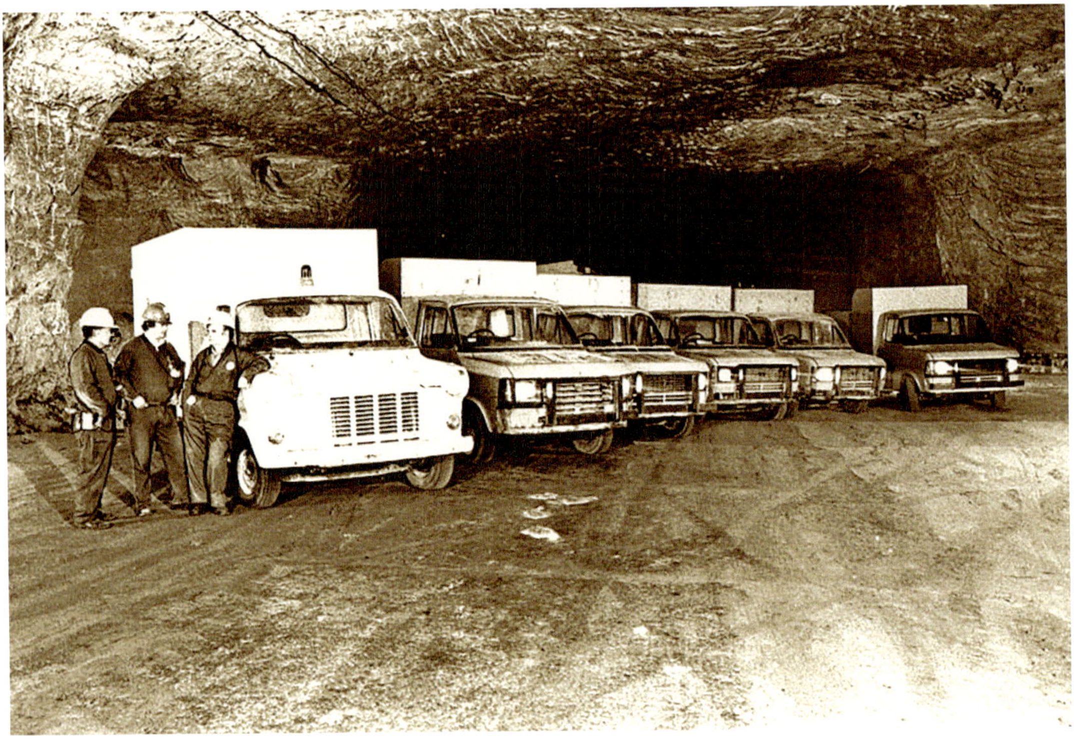

Winsford modern salt mine.

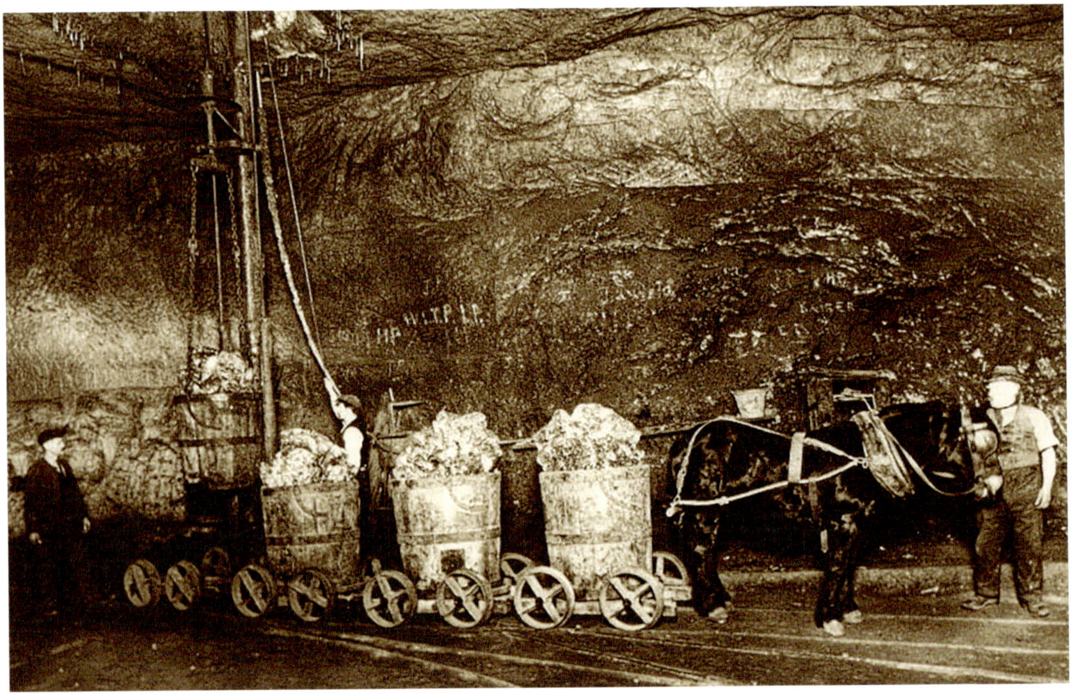

Old Northwich salt mine.

SALT MINING DAMAGE

J. Cumming Walters wrote in his book *Romantic Cheshire* in 1930:

> Northwich transports us at once to a goblin-realm of topsy-turveydom, and the stranger who finds himself amid the slanting structures has an impression at the outset of being involved in a crazy adventure. The natives are, of course, accustomed to walls askew, to sunken basements, squinting windows and bulging roofs. Whilst the stranger was seeing these things, the people of Northwich were continually propping up their buildings and remaining in them, even waking up in the morning and having to climb up out of the front door to leave the house.

It was a massive problem, unique in its effects upon the town, and something had to be done. The Verdin Trust was set up in 1889 by Sir Joseph Verdin to compensate people for subsidence caused by brine pumping. The charity, however, only ran for two years, for in 1891 the Brine Pumping Compensation Act came into force, rendering the trust redundant. Sir Joseph then used the collected money, along with some of his own, to build the Verdin Technical Schools at Winsford, which were opened in 1895. They were later extended to become Winsford Verdin Grammar School, which is now known as the currently closed Verdin Exchange. Adult education and small businesses occupied the premises. Also built with the funds was the Verdin Technical Schools in London Road, Northwich, in 1896, which later became the Art School and is now a residential building.

In the latter part of the nineteenth century, subsidence resulting from brine pumping was a significant issue, as is evident in the numerous photographs taken at the time and later. Many of these photographs were taken to document damage and support claims, but they have left us with a fine archive that shows just how much Northwich, and other areas, suffered in the late 1800s and into the next century.

In 1871, the Northwich Salt Chamber of Commerce requested that the Board of Trade investigate the problem and report back. This was done, and two years later their report concluded that the brine pumpers caused the subsidence damage and that they were responsible.

Accordingly, the Brine Pumping (Compensation for Subsidence) Act 1891 came into force and provided for the setting up of compensation boards. They had the power to collect a levy of 3*d* per 1,000 gallons of brine pumped within their district. They assessed the claims for damage caused by brine extraction. This Act specifically excluded any companies that profited

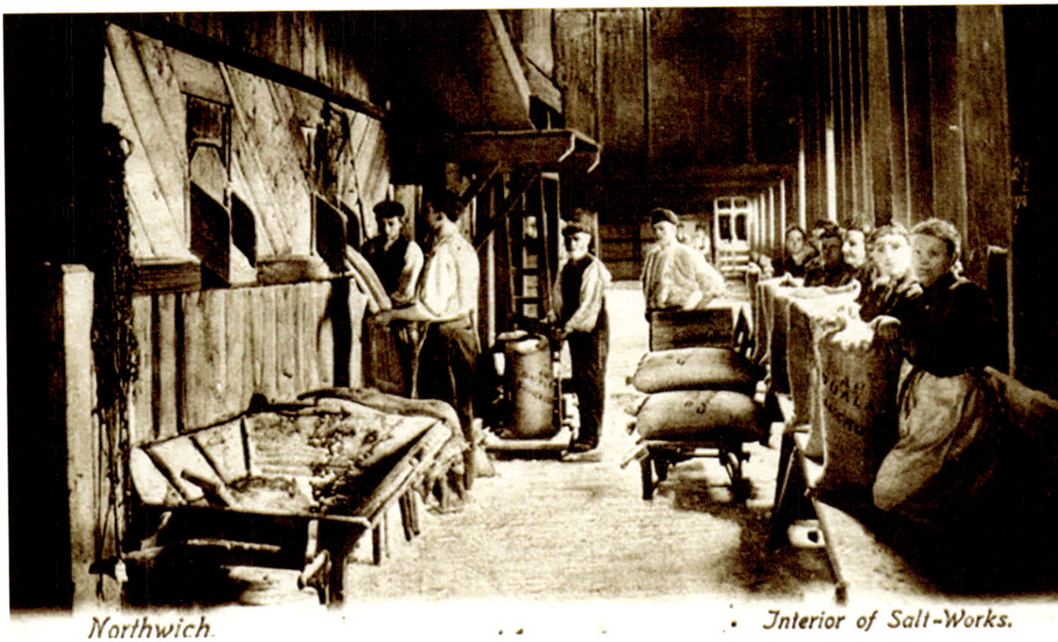

Northwich salt mine packing room.

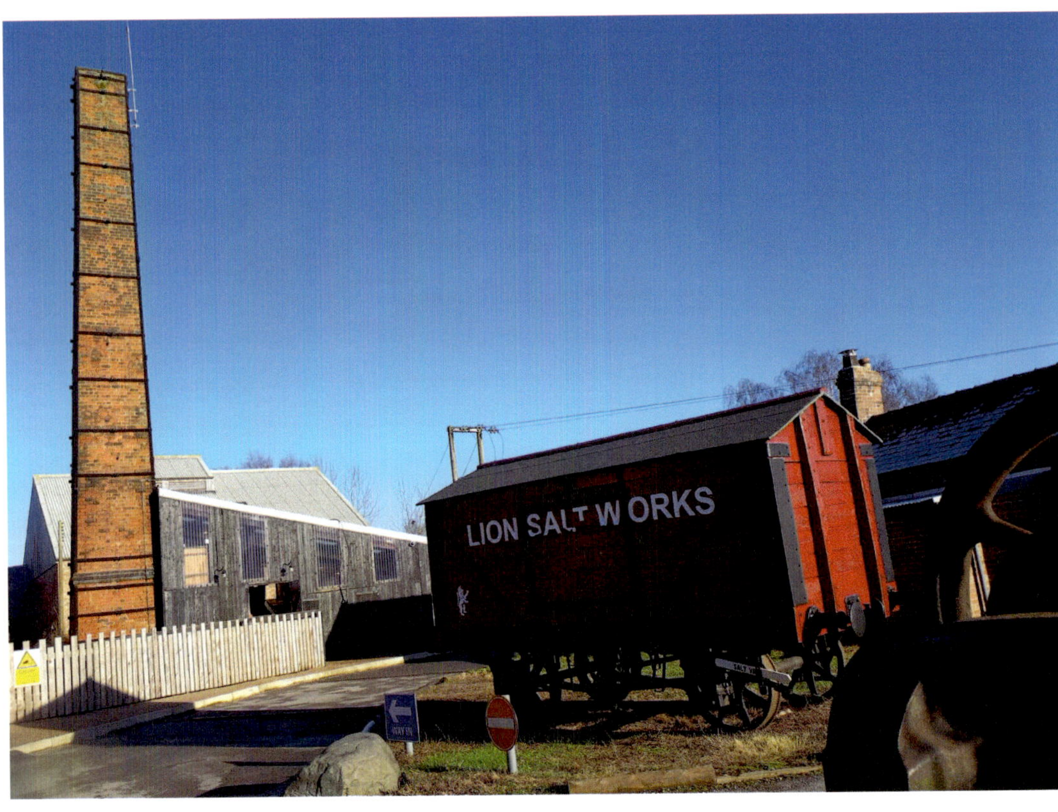

Lion Salt Works Museum.

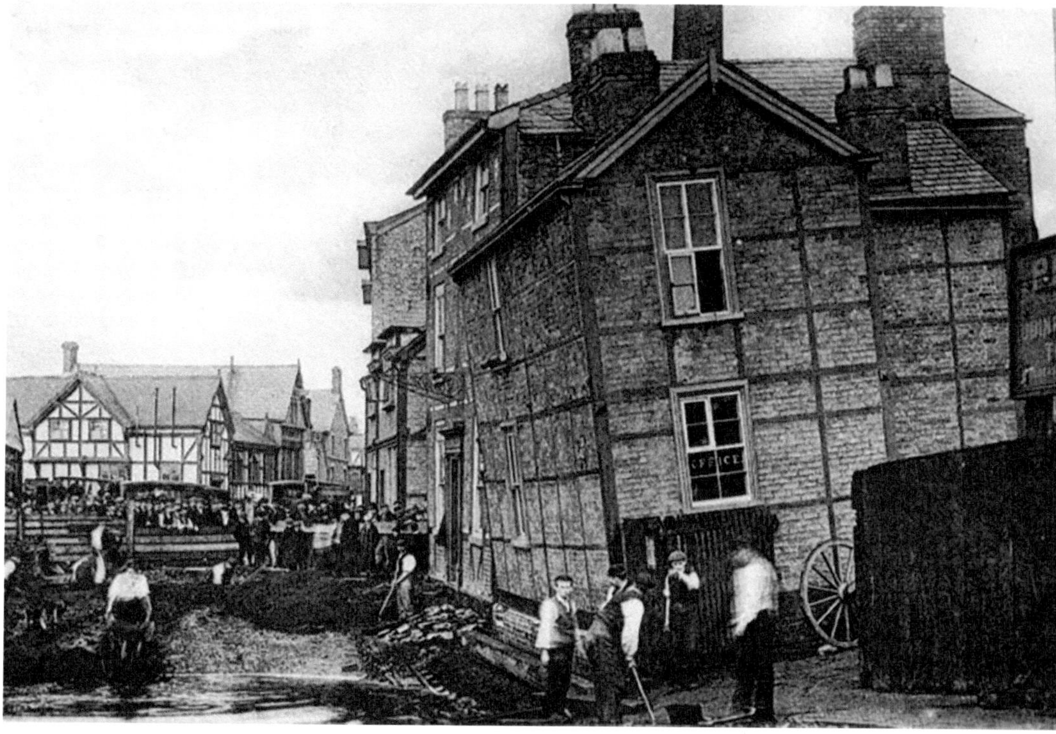

Subsided buildings.

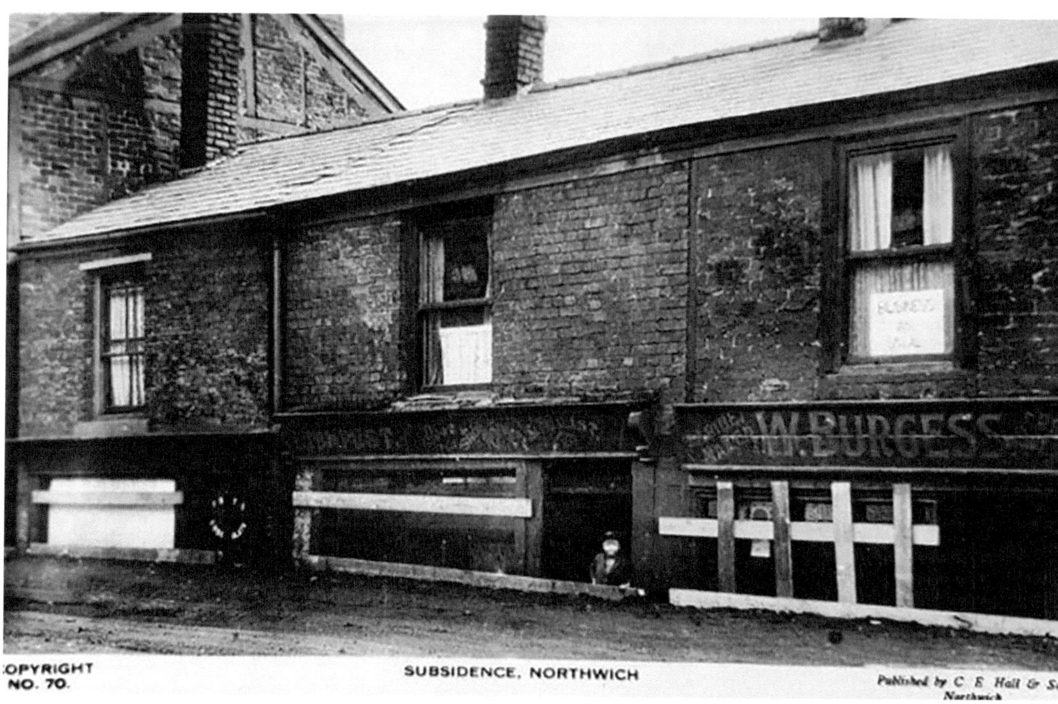

Subsided buildings.

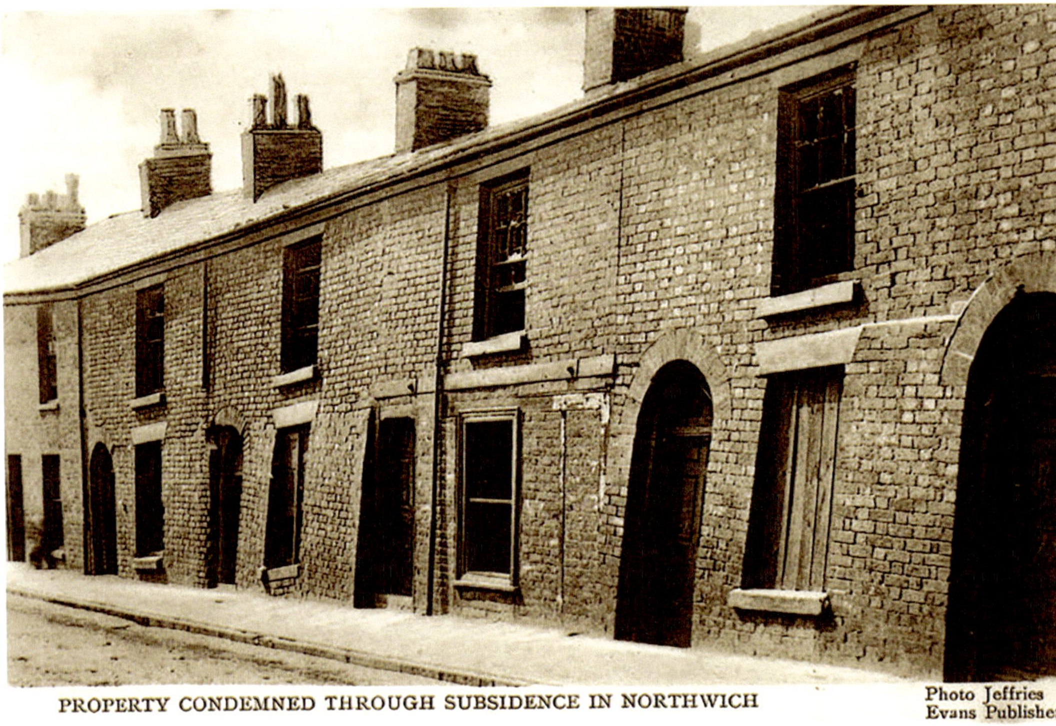

Property condemned due to subsidence.

directly or indirectly from the salt trade from claiming compensation. Only one compensation board was established for the Northwich district. Over the following years, salt extraction was more carefully monitored, and the Brine Compensation Board paid out any claims.

In 1952, it was time for a change, and the government passed the Cheshire Brine Pumping (Compensation for Subsidence) Act 1952, which created a single Compensation District covering the whole of Cheshire in areas where subsidence could occur. Nantwich was an exception as it declined to take part in the scheme. The Act was like the 1891 Act, under which a maximum levy of 6*d* per 1,000 gallons of brine pumped could be imposed on each brine pumper. A rebate came into force where controlled methods of pumping were used, mainly causing no additional damage. The same rules applied to brine pumpers, who could not claim compensation for damage to their own property, except for damage to houses owned by local authorities.

The Compensation Board, in consultation with the Planning Authority and Business Control, defined certain areas known to be at risk as Yellow or Consultation Areas.

Applications relating to the erection of buildings within these Yellow Areas could be declined planning permission as a result, especially if they were to be constructed without the structural precautions based on advice from the board. The 1952 Act was updated by the Brine Pumping (Compensation for Subsidence) Act 1964.

By the 1990s, Vale Royal Borough Council (VRBC) discovered that Northwich was still sinking, mainly due to the existence of redundant mines, and work was required to infill at least four of them: Witton Hall Mine, Penny's Lane Mine, Newmans Mine, and the largest, sited in the town centre, Barons Quay Mine, which was better known as the Leicester

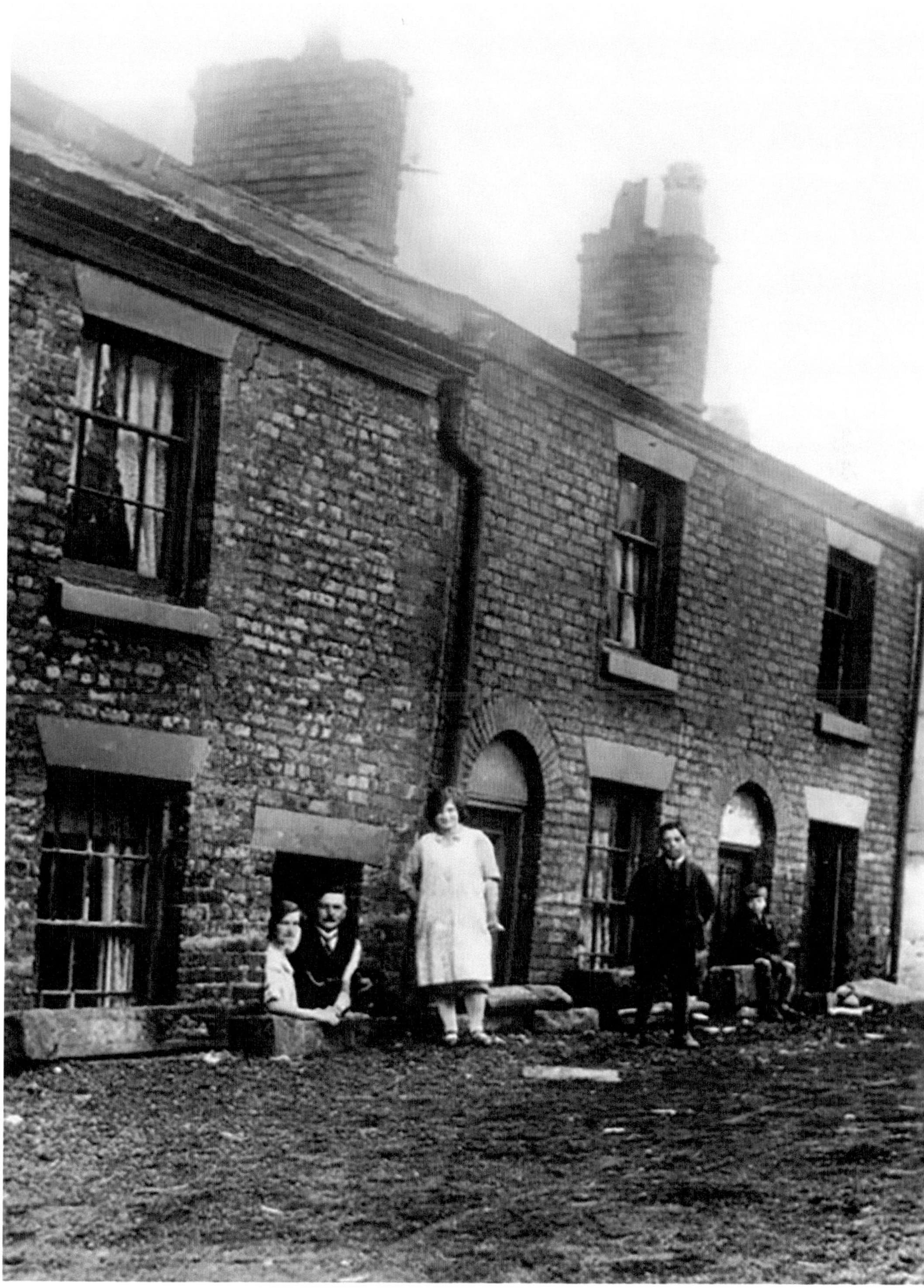

Subsided homes.

Street Mine. Accordingly, no further development was allowed in the town centre, seriously damaging Northwich's plans. VRBC applied for funding to English Partnerships as part of the government's Land Stabilisation Programme. As a result, they received funding for the project to infill the four mines, ensuring the stability of the town centre and allowing development. It became the largest project of its kind in the world when 780,500 cubic metres of void, 90 metres below ground, were to be filled with a mix of pulverised fuel ash grout. Due to the infill being in a rock salt area, the ash grout was to be mixed with brine to prevent it from dissolving.

The project cost £38 million, with English Partnerships paying £33 million and VRBC paying £5 million. As a result, Northwich was able to develop Barons Quay, featuring shops, entertainment venues and a cinema.

The Northwich Salt Mines Stabilisation Project received five awards, as follows.

- Most Innovative Remedial Method 2006
- Innovation Remediation 2006
- Regional Monitor Excellence 2007
- Ground Engineering Sustainability 2008
- ICE North West Merit 2008

By 23 October 2006, the Brine Pumping (Compensation for Subsidence) Act 1964 was amended and incorporated to cover damage caused by mining for coal and brine, as approved by the Law Society, and referred to as the Con29M mining search. Also, from 1 June 2018, the Cheshire Brine Compensation Board was renamed 'The Cheshire Salt Search'.

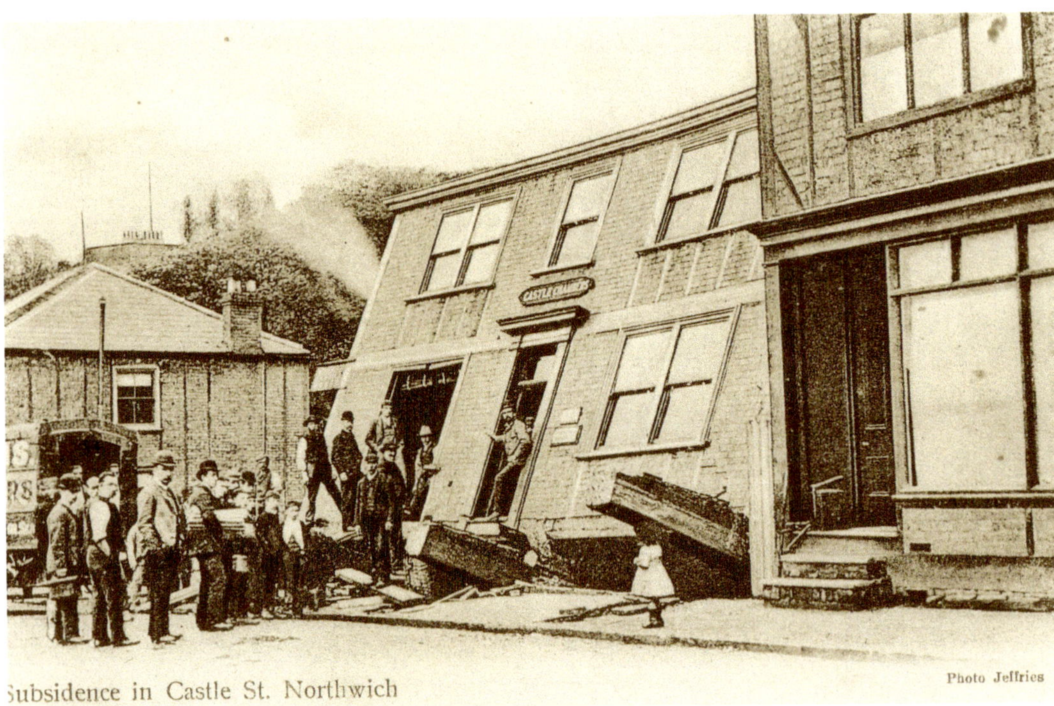

Subsidence in Castle Street.

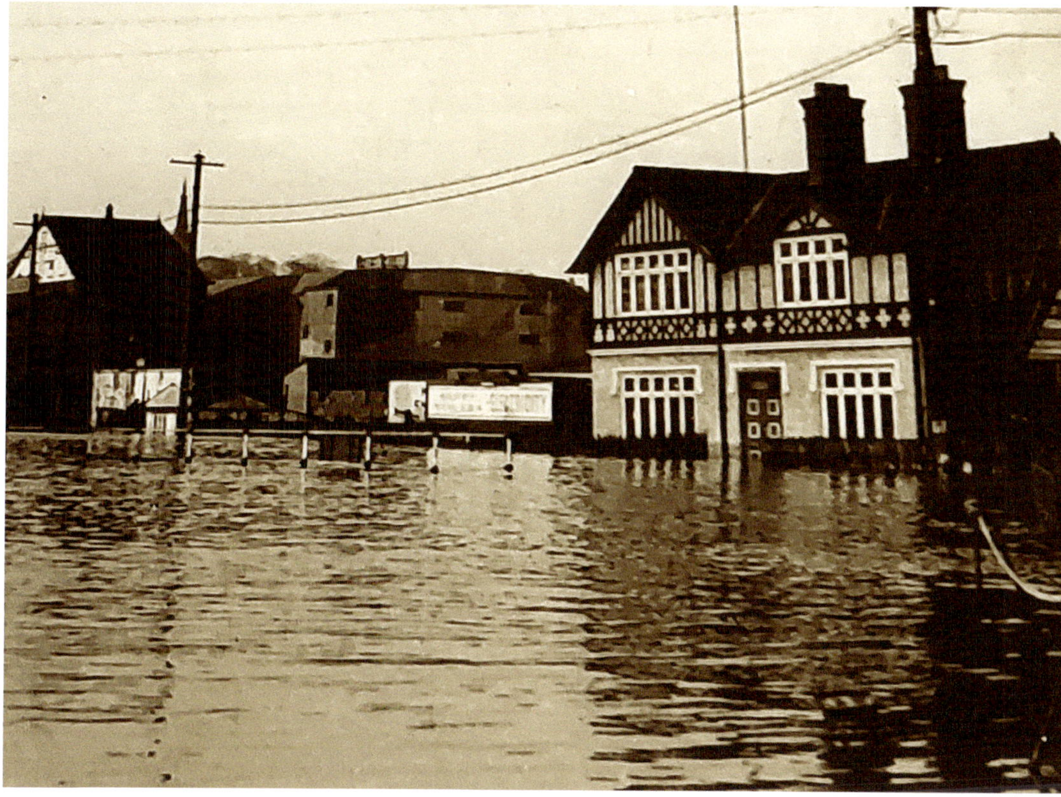

Brine Compensation Office, Northwich.

NORTHWICH SHIPBUILDERS

Despite being well inland, Northwich was famous for shipbuilding for many years, but it is no longer. Its firm W. J. Yarwood & Sons Ltd, from 1896 to 1966, built 1,000 vessels, including coasters, tugs, river and canal boats, and small military ships. Lawrence of Arabia spent time there in 1934 designing the RAF rescue craft *Aquarius*.

Isaac Pimblott & Sons was the second Northwich boatyard to also build small river and ocean craft, including torpedo boats and other warships during the Second World War. They traded from 1867 to 1974. Both companies have now gone, although their products can still be found around the world.

W. J. Yarwood's was formed by William James Yarwood (1851–1926), who served an apprenticeship in the iron foundry of William J. Bates & Son of Northwich and was later appointed as a blacksmith with the River Weaver Navigation.

He eventually became a foreman in the engineering department, working with notable engineers including Edward Leader Williams, who was designing the Manchester Ship Canal together with three eminent engineers, J. Watt Sandeman, L. B. Wells and Col J. A. Saner, who created the unique swing bridges for Northwich and several other locations, such as Acton Bridge and Stockton Heath.

The River Weaver had been canalised in 1721 under the Weaver Navigation Act. By then, salt had been rediscovered, and the Weaver provided an excellent way of transporting the salt to Liverpool. William Yarwood was involved in straightening and deepening it, and in building larger locks to enable larger ships to reach Northwich and Winsford.

In 1840, a Macclesfield gentleman by the name of John Thompson rented a piece of land in Navigation Road, Northwich. He set up a company building canal barges and sailing flats. These vessels had to be launched sideways because the river was too narrow at that point. During Thompson's tenure, the most notable ship built was the *Herald of Peace*, which was later sold to the Salt Union.

Thompson retired in 1885, and the business was taken over by a local man, John Woodcock. He had worked as a foreman at what was then named 'The Dock'. After eight years in that capacity, he purchased the business from John Thompson upon the latter's retirement. The company was a success, providing the Brunner Mond steamship *Cambria*, which worked the river until 1967, and *Scotia*, which also remained in service on the River Weaver until 1967.

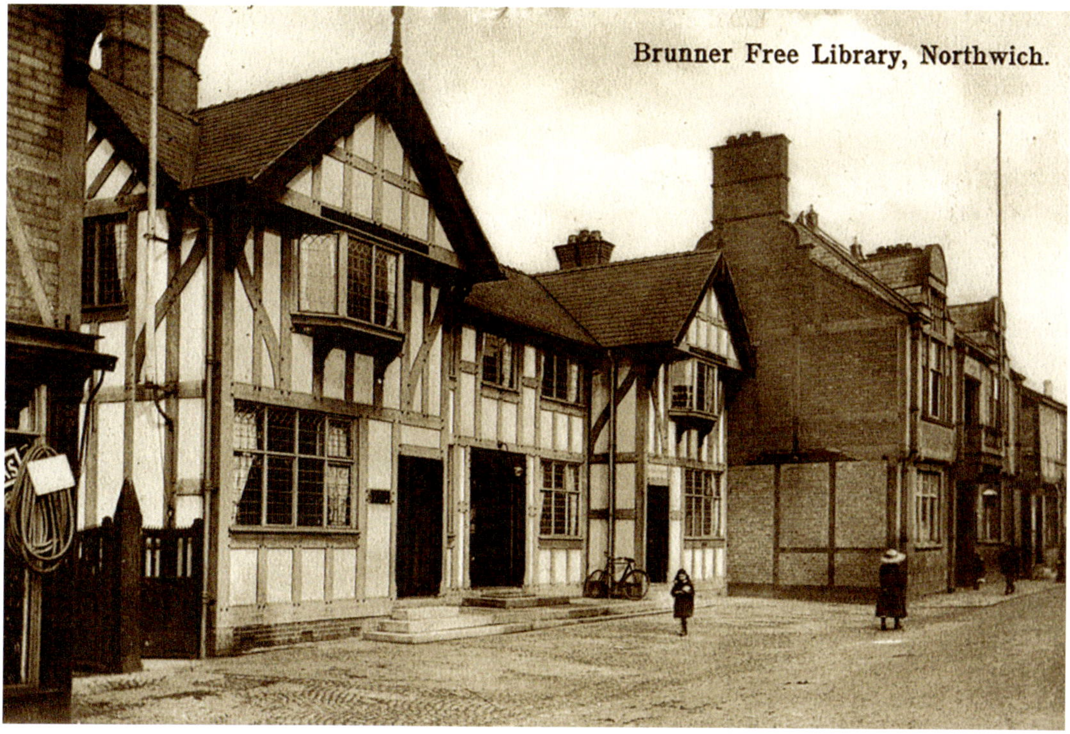

Northwich Library, *c.* 1920s.

Colin Stewart Minerals of Winsford eventually took these over. Brunner Mond ordered a prototype steamship, *Hibernia*, but unfortunately, during the build, John Woodcock suddenly died, and William James Yarwood was contracted to finish the job. He did so still in his capacity of foreman, but in charge of the work on 'The Dock' until 1896, when he became owner. His past qualifications as a blacksmith and shipbuilder made him the ideal person to take over 'The Dock'.

In the early 1870s, William met and married Mary Anne Holgrave of Liverpool, and they raised a family of four sons and two daughters. His boys were able to join him in the business. They were Albert (1877–1975), Enoch Henry (1879–1950), Sydney (1886–1969) and William Douglas (1892–1990). By 1905, the business was called W. J. Yarwood & Son. Five years later, it became W. J. Yarwood & Sons Ltd. With his sons holding positions in the company, William was able to engage in civic duties. He became a JP, chairman of the council, and had many other posts, including being appointed a trustee of the River Weaver Navigation.

In its first three years, the new company had delivered fifteen vessels to the Manchester Ship Canal Company, Douglas Corporation in the Isle of Man, and Brunner Mond. Later vessels were delivered to the Admiralty, the Air Ministry, the Mersey Docks and Harbour Board, and canal-carrying companies, including the Grand Union Canal Carrying Company and Fellows Morton and Clayton. The new company had hit the ground running.

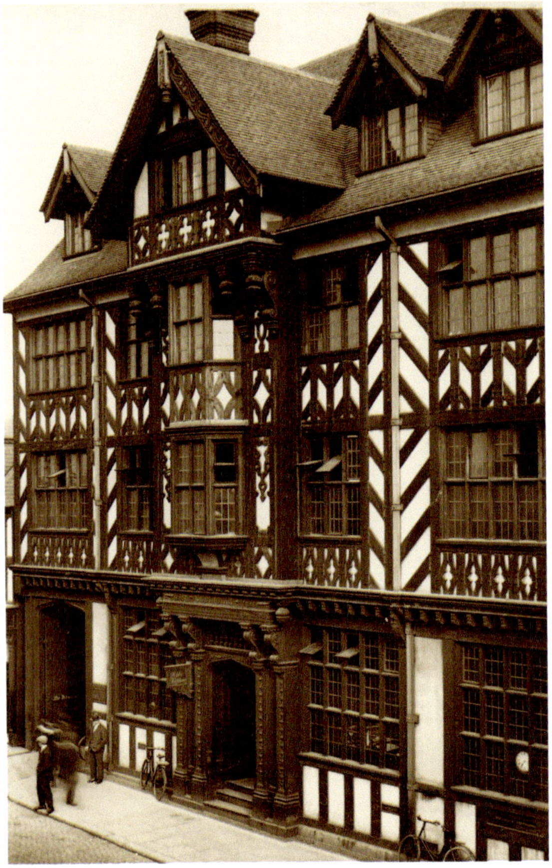

Northwich Post Office, now a Wetherspoon's.

ROYAL NAVY AVIATION FUEL LIGHTER

No photograph but one of several lighters built by Yarwood for the Royal Navy during the Second World War, the C626 was 150 feet long and was tasked as an aviation fuel lighter when completed in 1943. It continued in that role for about forty years. In 1985, it was selected for conversion to the training ship *Ajax*, serving HMS Raleigh at Torpoint, Cornwall. In this task, it replaced the frigate HMS *Ajax*. Its role continued until February 2008, when it was withdrawn and offered for sale at £95,000. It has been converted into a houseboat at Shoreham.

Safe Hand had the last steam engine built for service on the Mersey and became the last steam vessel in service with the Lever Brothers fleet. It was built in 1950 by Yarwood's as the steam tank barge *Lux* for Lever Brothers, to carry crude vegetable oils from the Mersey ports to Lever's facility at Port Sunlight. In February 1965, it was converted to diesel at Birkenhead and continued to work for Lever Brothers until December 1984. It was renamed *Safe Hand* in 1975. Its cargo-carrying facilities comprise two tanks, capable of storing vegetable oils in the Liverpool and Birkenhead docks, and is still in service.

Let us look at a warship that Yarwood's built. HMS *Marlingford*, a fast patrol boat launched on 17 June 1954, saw minimal service, being in reserve at Barrow for some time. It was sold for disposal to Pounds of Portsmouth on 8 September 1967.

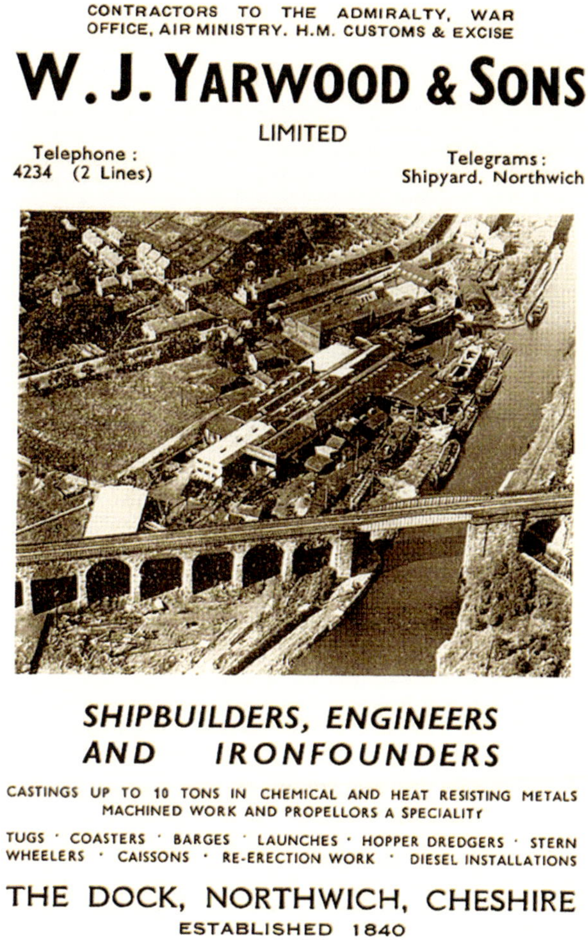

Yarwood advert.

Another ship of note was the *Aquarius*, famous by virtue of the fact that one of those present at the building was Lawrence of Arabia. It was built as a rescue vessel for downed pilots, but it had a tragic ending. After launching, *Aquarius* eventually made a 9,000-mile maiden voyage to Singapore to serve as a depot ship for flying boats. Later, when Singapore fell to the Japanese in 1942, *Aquarius* escaped and was probably making for Australia. Lloyd's War Losses states: 'About 14 February 1942, *Aquarius* was sunk off the southeast coast of Sumatra, on board were 60 to 70 persons, of which only three survived, and these also subsequently died.'

The largest ship built at the W. J. Yarwood's boatyard was *Athelbrae*, an oil or molasses tanker launched on 24 March 1955 for the Athel Line, a subsidiary of United Molasses. Due to the vessel's size, it was damaged during launch and is seen here on its way to the Mersey for repair.

The tanker was in service until at least 1971/72 and was sold to the government of Guyana in 1977. In 1979, it was beached on the Essequibo River for scrapping, which took place on 1 January 1982. Athelbrae Close in Northwich is named after the ship.

The last vessel to leave the company was the 68-ton diesel tug *St Elmo*, built for work in Valletta Harbour, Malta. The W. J. Yarwood & Sons Ltd company no longer exists, and the buildings have been demolished; the land has been put to other uses.

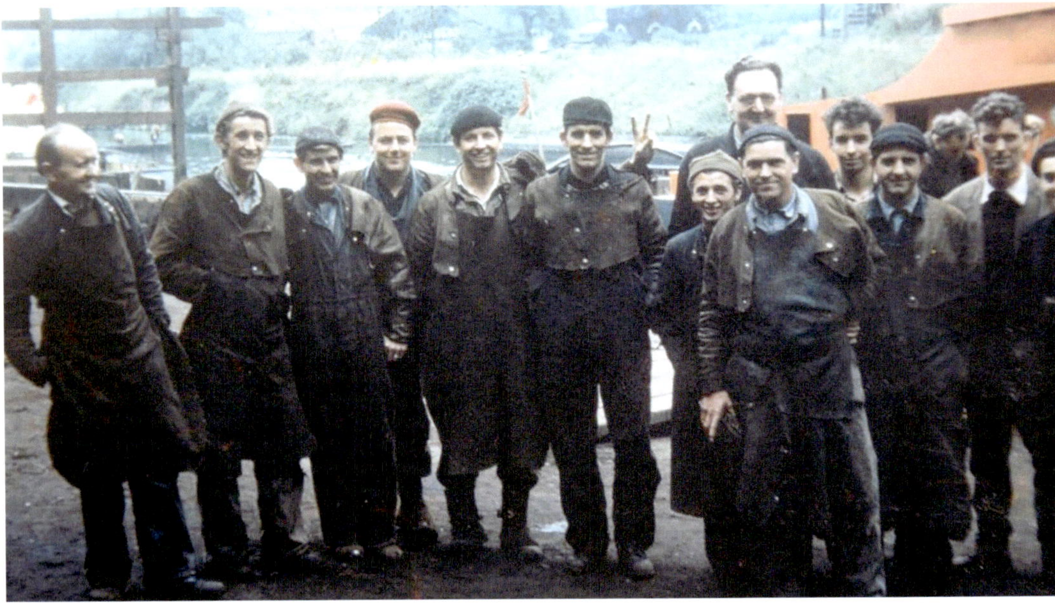

Group of Yarwood employees. (Source: *Northwich Guardian*)

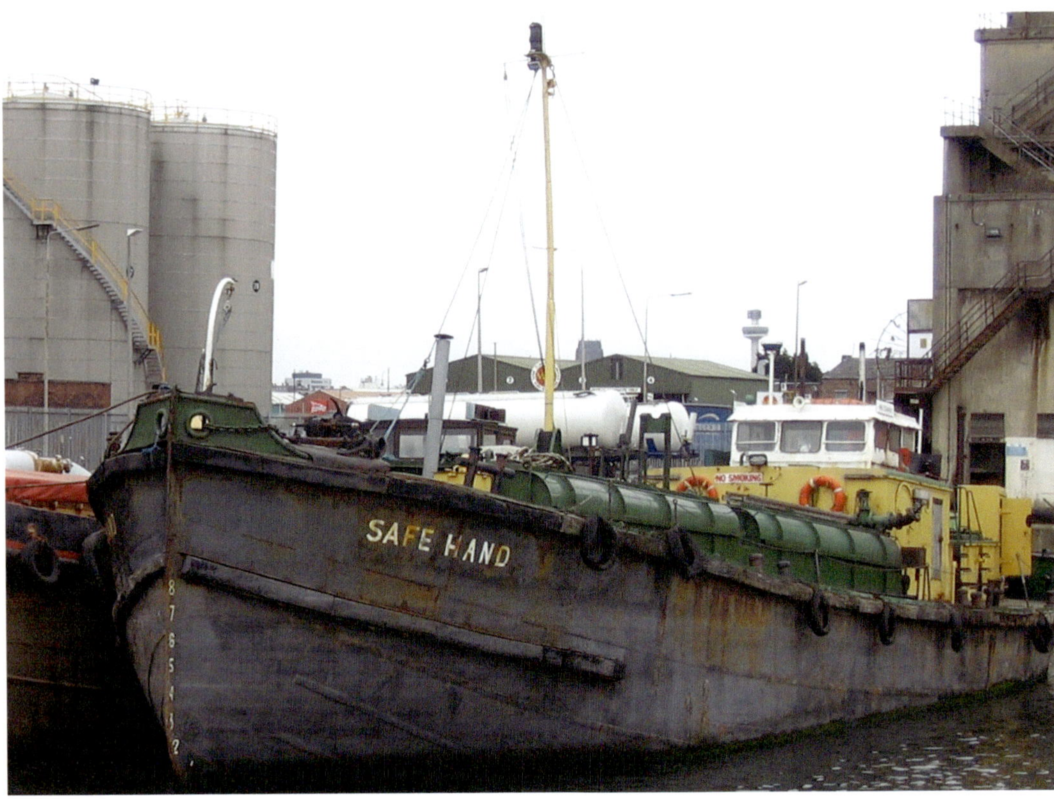

Safe Hand, built by Yarwood's in 1950. (Source: Paul Brown, *Historic Ships: The Survivors* (Amberley Publishing))

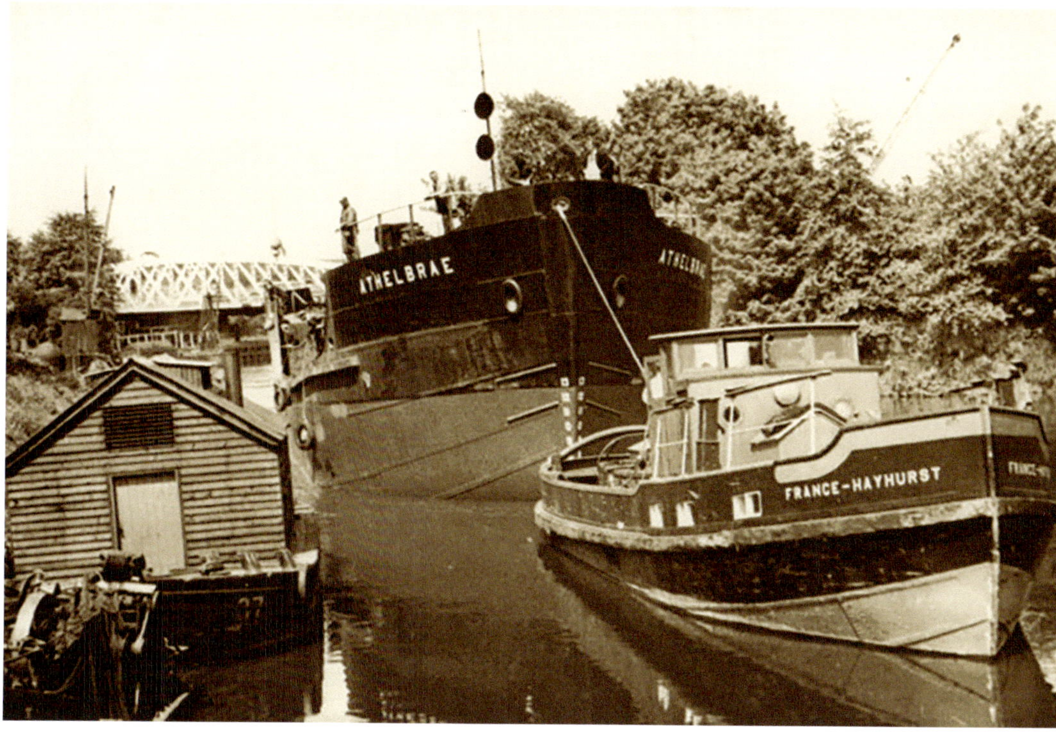

Athelbrae passing Acton Bridge. (Source: W. J. Yarwood)

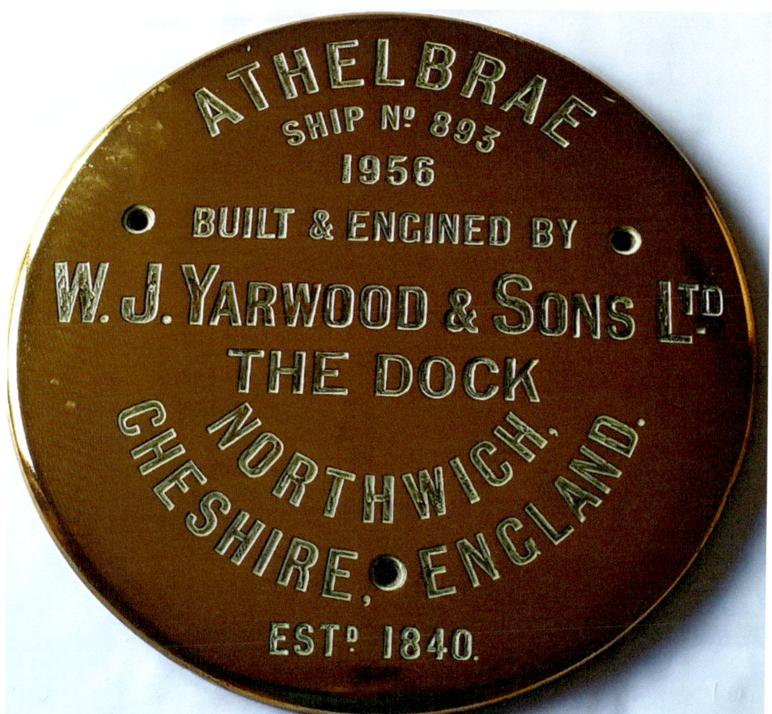

Athelbrae builders' plaque.

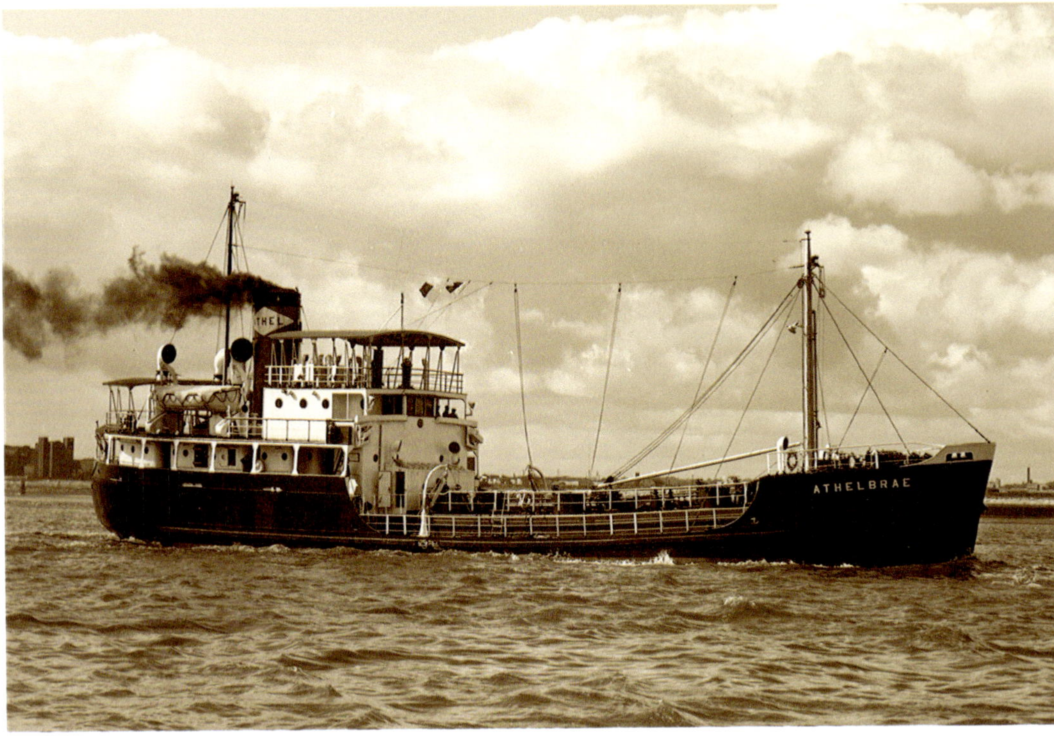

Athelbrae at sea when repaired.

ISAAC PIMBLOTT AND SONS

The inland town of Northwich housed two shipbuilding companies, the second of which was Isaac Pimblott and Sons. The shipbuilding company was founded in 1867 by Isaac Pimblott, born on 10 May 1844 to a humble family and residing in New Street, Northwich.

Isaac gained experience working at Joseph Parks in Northwich and Vernon's shipyard in Liverpool. When he returned to Northwich, he founded Pimblott's Shipyard near Hayhurst Bridge on the River Weaver, later moving further upstream. He died on 19 January 1904.

One ship built of note was P3124, HMS *Montford*, a fast patrol boat that was launched on 10 October 1957. It was a member of a class of fast patrol boats built for the Royal Navy in the 1950s. All had the last name 'Ford', hence the Ford Class of ships. On 9 September 1966, it was sold to Nigeria and renamed NNS *Ibadan*. When the Biafrans declared independence, it was captured by them in Calabar. Under the Biafran flag, it saw action as BNS *Vigilance* against the Nigerians during the Civil War and on 9 October 1967, it was sunk in Port Harcourt near the oil depot of Bonny in the Niger Delta.

The Pimblott's yard closed in 1971 and went into voluntary liquidation in 1972. A marina now covers the site.

ASSORTED NORTHWICH BUSINESSES

John Kerr and Company (Manchester) was a manufacturer of fire protection, from fire engines to hoses and buckets. It was the parent company of Davy Automatic Fire Escapes, based in London Road, Northwich.

The John Kerr Company was established in 1908 as John Kerr McMyn, specialising in fire prevention and firefighting. From 1903 to the present day, the company has undergone several mergers and acquisitions, and it is now part of the Kidde company, which continues to operate within the firefighting industry.

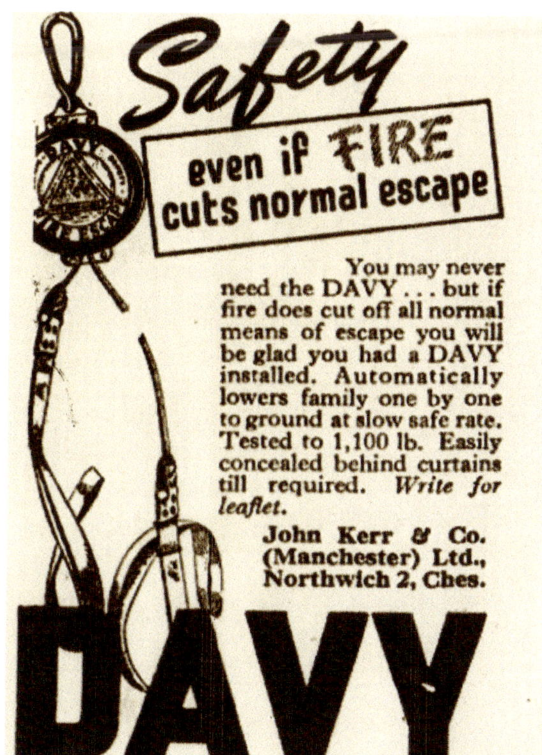

Davy company advert. (Source: 1943 *Countryman*)

This equipment was initially invented in the USA and manufactured by John Kerr. The Davy Fire Escape business sold it in Northwich. John Kerr used the business name 'Kerko' and had the Northwich address. The method of use was to bolt it to the wall near a high window, behind the curtains. Should escape from a fire be needed, people could be lowered to the ground using it. It was manufactured and sold until quite recently as a Davy Descender sold by Safelincs. It has now been discontinued.

DUTTON'S LEATHER WORKS

The firm of Dutton and Lamb was founded in 1809 and engaged in all forms of leatherwork. In 1870, the partnership was dissolved, and the business continued as George Dutton and Sons, Weaver Leather Works, Northwich. They were engaged in producing leathers for cotton spinning, hat leathers, skivers (the carved leather found set into desktops, especially in the early days), and shoe leathers. The 1911 census records that father Joseph Frederick Dutton and son George Frederick Dutton were both employed at the leather manufacturers at the Weaver Leather Works and living at No. 142 London Road, Leftwich.

Weaver Leather Works was situated just on the Northwich side of the London Road railway arches. It covered 3 acres, employed eighty, and was one of the oldest such businesses in the trade.

It remained in the Dutton family. Joseph Dutton was succeeded by his son, William Dutton, and his grandson, George Dutton, and brother-in-law, William Lamb. In 1920, it became a limited company known as George Dutton and Sons, Northwich. The Tan Yard burned down in 1965. The current site on London Road is now used as a small industrial complex called Duttons Business Centre – a hark back to its previous occupants.

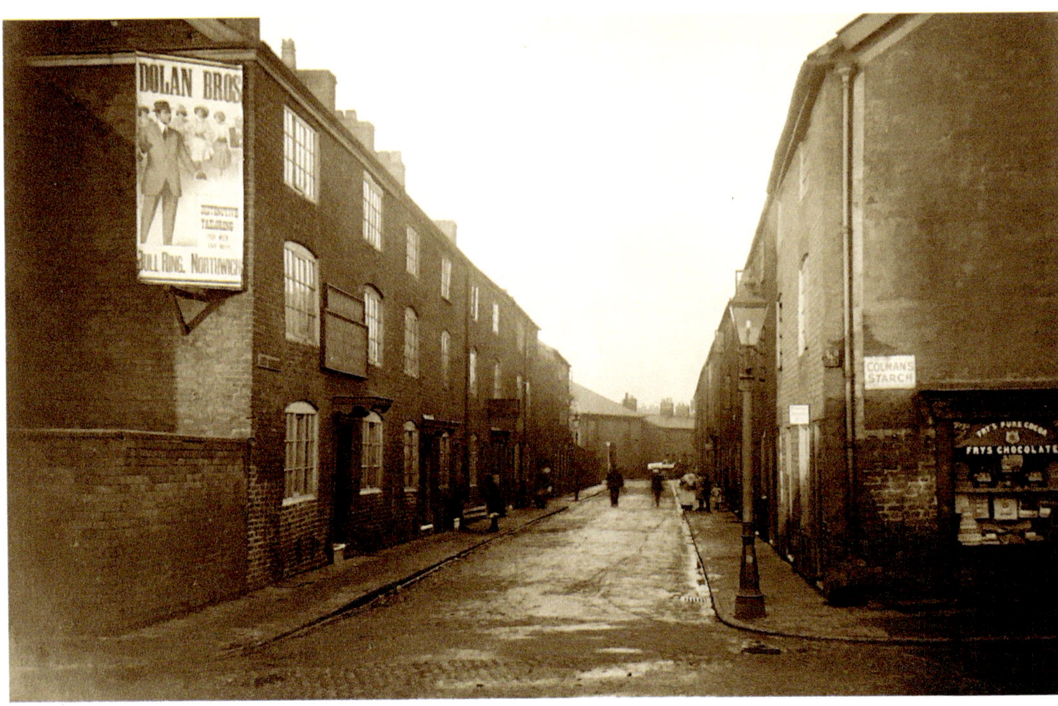

New Street, Northwich.

INTERNATIONAL TOXIN PRODUCTS (ITP)

This Northwich company, which sold fertiliser for farms and gardens, had a postal address at The Heysoms, No. 163 Chester Road, Northwich. It dates back to 1935 and was recognised as the leading lawn specialist in the country. Customers included the Royal Lawns at Ascot racecourse, where their product, 'Velvetone', had been used for many years, and the lawns at Oxford and Cambridge colleges. The Inner Temple gardens were maintained with Floratone and Velvetone, making their lawns one of the most attractive features of the London Embankment. In the sports world, the lawns at Wimbledon and the cricket grounds at Lord's and the Oval benefited from the use of ITP products. The grass at many bowling greens, including the oldest bowling green in the country at Southampton, was conditioned with Velvetone in the days when many insecticides were considered dangerous. ITP was a pioneer in the discovery of derris as a safe insecticide.

The factory was situated in Vearows Place off Queen Street in Northwich. The council created a new access road from the factory, providing them with good access to Queen Street.

When ITP relocated from The Heysoms, No. 163 Chester Road, the building eventually became Haysoms College in the 1920s to 1940s and later the Odiyana Kadampa Buddhist Meditation Centre.

International Toxin Products (ITP) was a company that produced industrial and agricultural chemical products, including disinfectants, pest control products, and veterinary treatments. The company was also known as Quantum International Products Ltd.

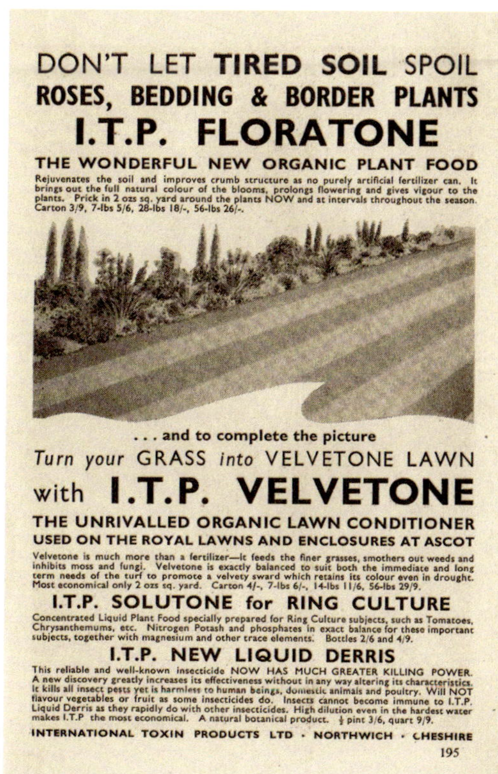

ITP advert from the 1943 *Countryman* magazine. (Source: 1943 *Countryman*)

JABEZ THOMPSON (1838–1911) TERRACOTTA WORKS

The word terracotta means 'fired earth'. In architecture, it typically refers to a type of masonry made from moulded clay, often larger than brick and of finer quality. When glazed, it is known as 'faience'. Terracotta became popular in this country in the 1860s, when it became more cost-effective following mass production. It provided another dimension to architectural style and decoration. The influence came from Ancient Greek temples and Italian Renaissance churches favoured by the Victorians. Moulds were made depicting these images. Until then, stonework had been used to adorn buildings, but this was expensive. Terracotta provided a far cheaper alternative to stone. It was used extensively on the external façades of the Royal Albert Hall and the Victoria and Albert Museum, both in London, in the 1860s. The choice of terracotta in the construction of these buildings increased its popularity. In 1867, Sir Charles Barry presented a report to the Royal Institute of British Architects extolling its virtues. Terracotta was light and easy to transport; it was strong in compression; it was a cheaper material than stone, as it did not require hand carving; and it had a smooth, fired surface that was more dirt-resistant than stone, an essential consideration in the dirty atmosphere of Victorian Britain.

Jabez Thompson, the ninth son of John Thompson Senior (1799–1867), employed terracotta in Northwich. In the 1860s, the Thompsons had two family businesses: the Alliance Salt Works and the terracotta brickworks on Manchester Road, Northwich. In 1867, Jabez's father died and he inherited the terracotta brickworks, taking over the running of the brick and tile works in Northwich (first established in 1824), whilst his brothers ran the salt works.

Initially, the brickworks produced common, fine and moulded bricks. Bricks that can now be found after demolishing old buildings. Each one has the Jabez Thompson stamp. Jabez expanded the works and specialised in terracotta, including the production of panels and ornamental pieces. One such panel was the 'Last Supper' reredos, which was advertised in the *Nantwich Guardian* on 18 September 1880. One of these panels was paid for by Sir Gilbert and Lady Greenall to be installed in the St Michael and All Angels Church at Little Leigh, behind the altar. The church was designed by the Liverpool architect Edmund Kirby and built in 1878–79 by the Hartford contractor Richard Beckett. The design is in the Gothic Revival style, and it is today a Grade II listed building due to its special architectural and historic interest.

Terracotta facing bricks from the Northwich brickworks were used in the external and internal walls of the church. Internally, the walls were decorated with ornamental terracotta cornices and terracotta dressings, including the font, all of which complemented the terracotta reredos.

Examples of the company's terracotta works can be found above the door and the exterior wall panels at the old Art College on London Road (now flats), the front of the Beehive pub in High Street (now an estate agents) and the Winnington Cooperative building, to name but a few. (Source: Northwich Township heritage project)

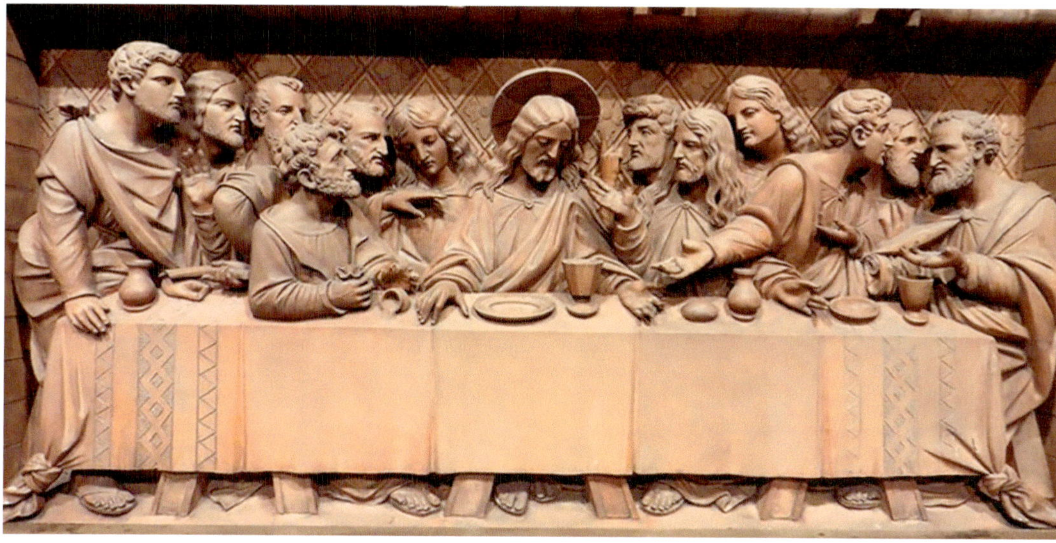

Jabez Thompson standard common brick.

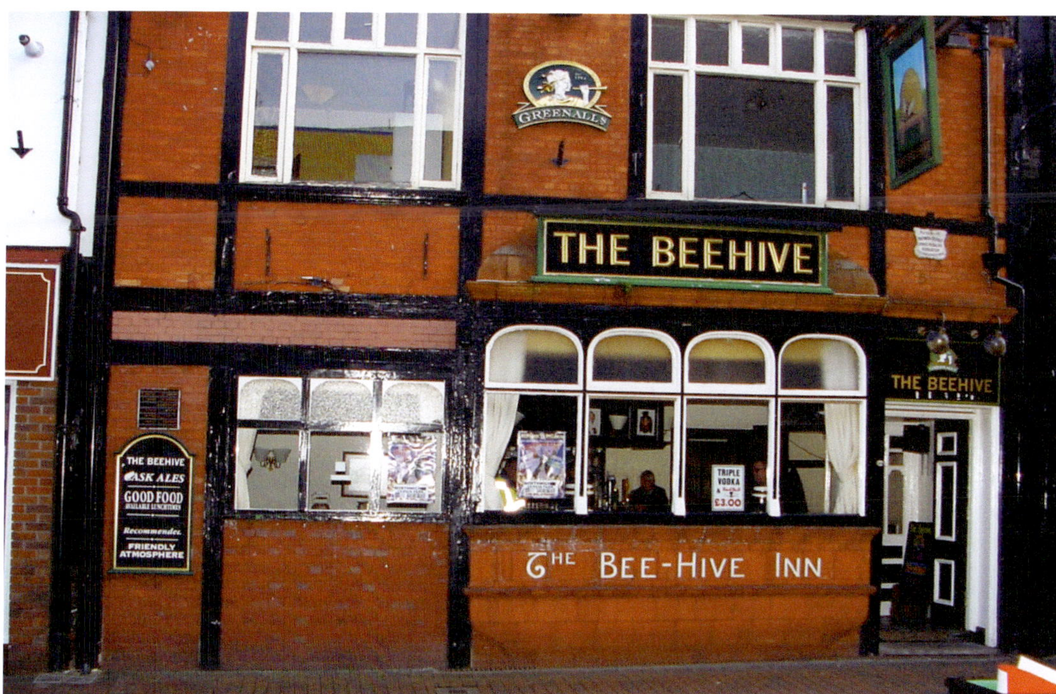

The Beehive public house.

NORTHWICH'S ICONIC BAKERIES

BROADHURST BAKERY

Earlier in this book, we looked at the massive explosion at the Brunner Mond works in Silvertown, London, caused by TNT and munitions work during the First World War. Here we look at the business that was situated in another of Brunner Mond's munitions factories. The works at Gadbrook, Rudheath, was also used to manufacture TNT after the loss of the Silvertown works. Fortunately, there was no explosion, unlike at Silvertown. However, some women who worked with the explosives suffered from orange/yellow-coloured skin caused by mixing the TNT and cordite by hand, which is what they did. Four hundred women in the country suffered from the work, 100 fatally.

There was a more positive use for the Gadbrook Munitions factory after the war. (The Gad Brook is the stream on the edge of the land.) Mr and Mrs William Broadhurst manufactured cakes in Warrington. The Broadhurst family had a history of baking dating back to the 1800s, but by 1928, William and his wife were searching for new premises.

They settled on the old munitions factory at Gadbrook, Rudheath, which, with its 23-acre site, was ideal for converting to a bakery. Their sons, Sidney, Herbert and Henry, were involved in the business, as were other relatives – it was a true family affair. The company was named Broadhurst & Co. (Gadbrook) Ltd.

It was later known as Cheshire's Garden Bakery, and its products included cakes, biscuits and, later, pies.

The business was an immediate success under the initial leadership of William Broadhurst, and by the start of the Second World War, Broadhurst and Co. (Gadbrook) Ltd employed around 500 people. They supplied their products across the north of England and North Wales, while also supplying the armed forces with cakes and biscuits, thereby aiding the war effort, later with a fleet of vans in their caramel-and-cream livery.

Over the years, the company has had a good reputation for taking care of its staff. Plenty of land was put to good use by providing a football and cricket pitch.

All sorts of sports, both indoors and out, were provided. In the late 1960s, the company opened a social club in the canteen block, assisted by Greenall Whitley, the brewer. A bar was provided in a room suitable for social events. It was called the Gadbrook Social and was run by two employees, Les Boney and Doug Hayes, with help from three other members,

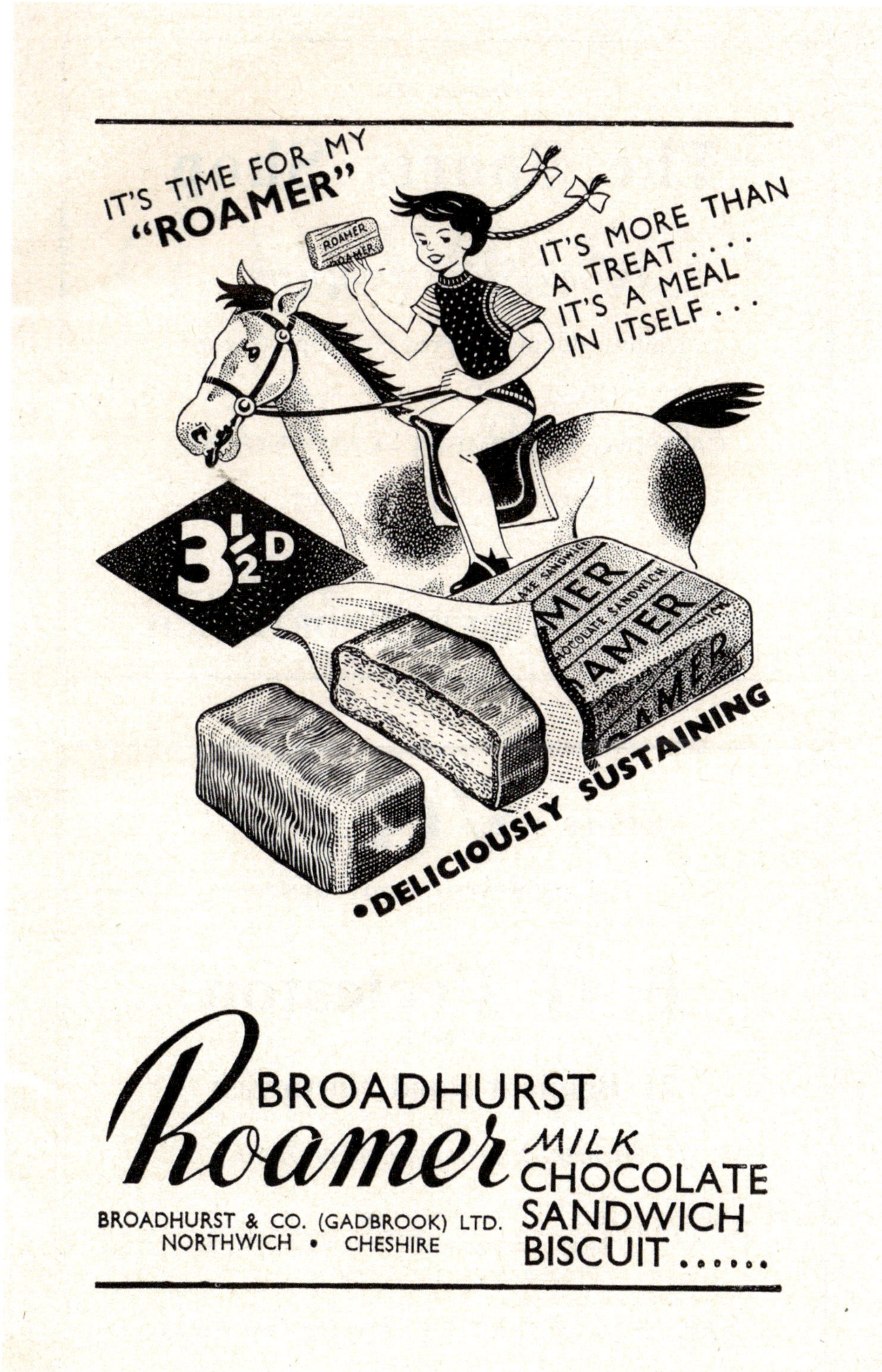

Broadhurst advert.

brothers Tommy, Colin and Cyril Leather. The company was acquired by Adams Foods, which subsequently closed the factory in 1987.

The land has now been redeveloped as a business park, known as the Gadbrook Park Development. (Source: Broadhurst archive)

ROBERTS BAKERY

Roberts Bakery now has 800 employees supplying top-quality bread to the UK and Europe, with sub-bakeries, including one in Derby. But where did it all start?

The story commences in the 1860s when Robert Roberts learnt his trade in Salford. He was just eleven years old when he began his apprenticeship in bread baking and groceries. Even at that young age, Robert was a bit of an entrepreneur and saw the possibilities that the trade offered him. In 1891, he had moved to Northwich and was a boarder with a family residing at No. 8 Navigation Road, Castle.

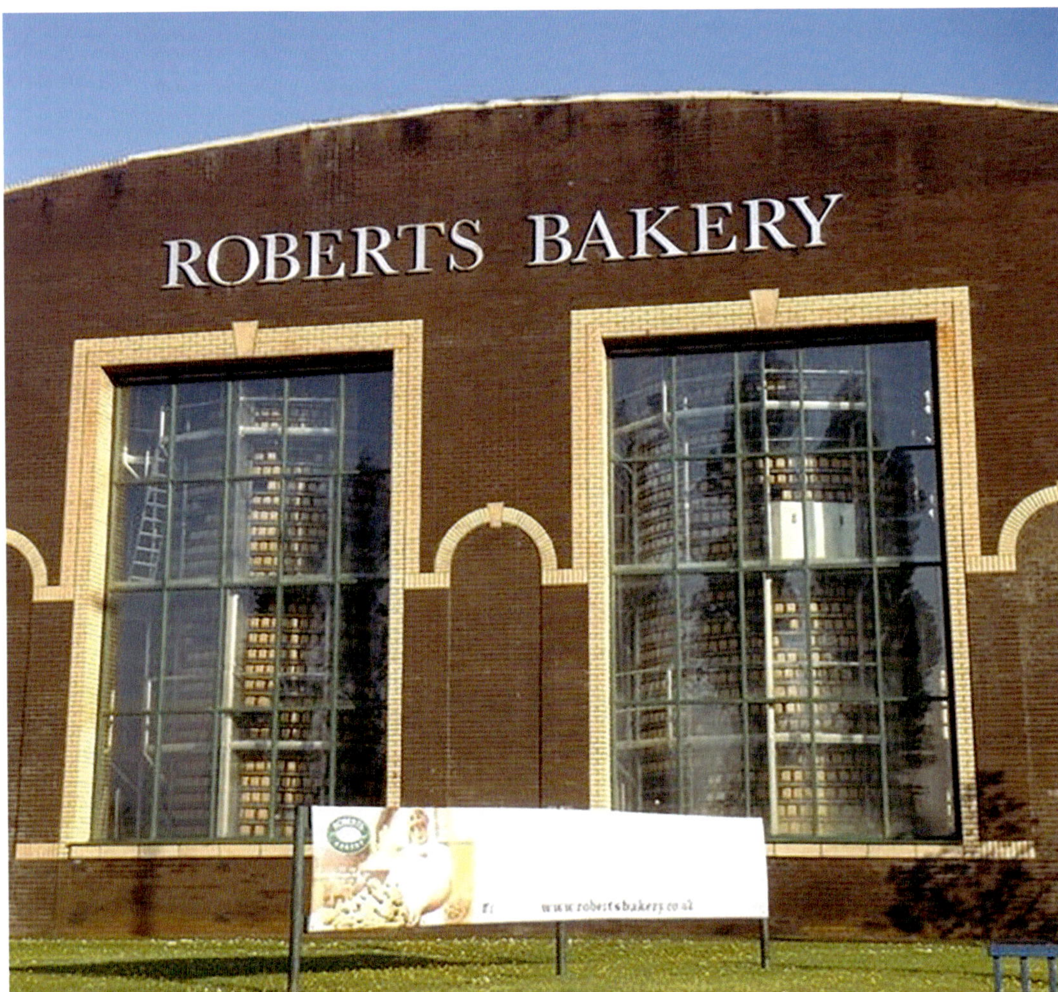

Roberts Bakery, the beginning.

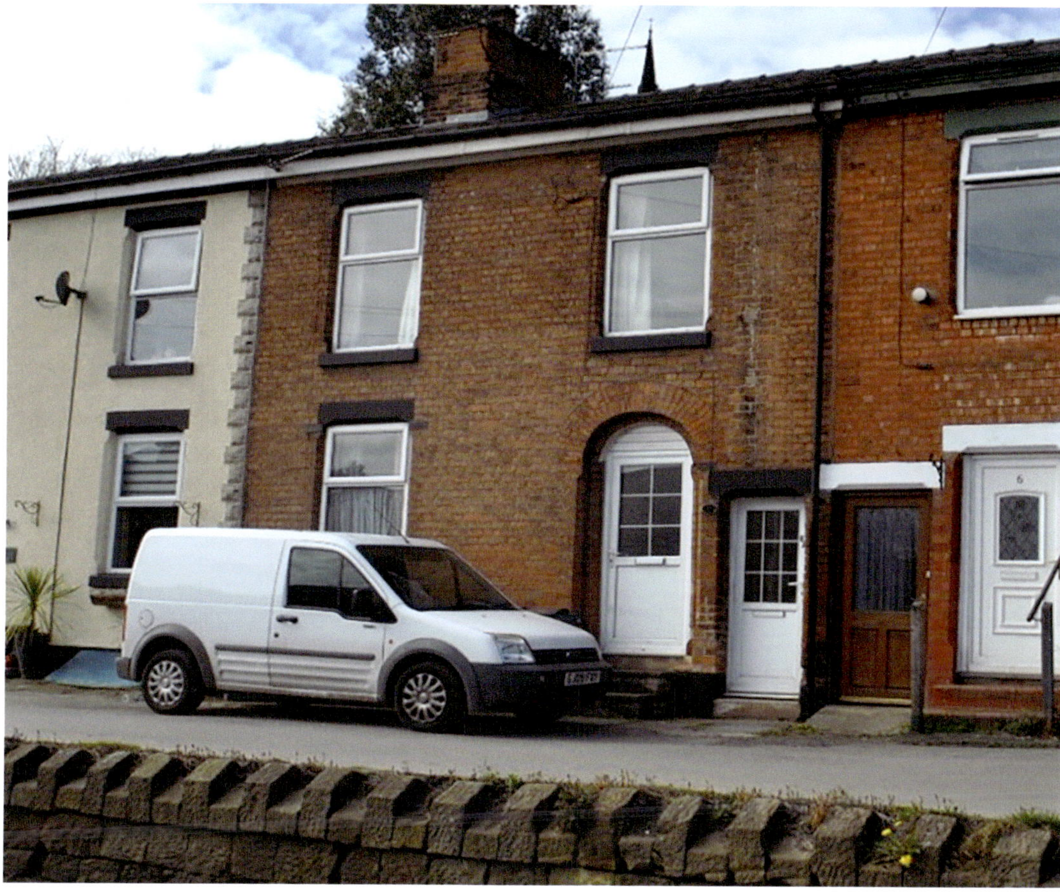

No. 8 Navigation Road, Northwich. (Source: author)

That family comprised Sarah Shaw, aged sixty, and her seven adult children; Robert was listed as a baker and provision dealer from Salford. In 1887, he had bought a grocery and fresh bread shop at No. 1 Wellington Street, Castle, now a private house, where he sold and delivered groceries and his homemade bread.

At the time, the street was a typical terraced street, and it still is today. In 1893, Robert Roberts married Mary Jane Gough from Byley. By 1901, he had moved his business to No. 26 Station Road, Lostock. The building still stands and is in use. The bakery and grocery store were a success, and by 1911, he had a thriving business that had expanded into the next-door property, No. 24.

Meanwhile, his son Frank, aged fifteen, was a boarder and a grocer's apprentice at No. 17 Green Lane, Wallasey. Over the next few years, Robert's wife, Mary, and their children – Frank, Annie, Alice, Ada and Nellie – worked in the business to varying degrees. It thrived, and in the 1920s, Robert modernised it with mechanisation, including bread slicers and fast-wrapping machines. In 1922, Frank married Jennie Pinkney, and they moved to Sunningdale, Manchester Road, Lostock Gralam.

In the 1930s, Frank Roberts became the managing director of the business and decided to concentrate on baking the best bread possible. The founder, Robert Roberts, died on 22 July 1936,

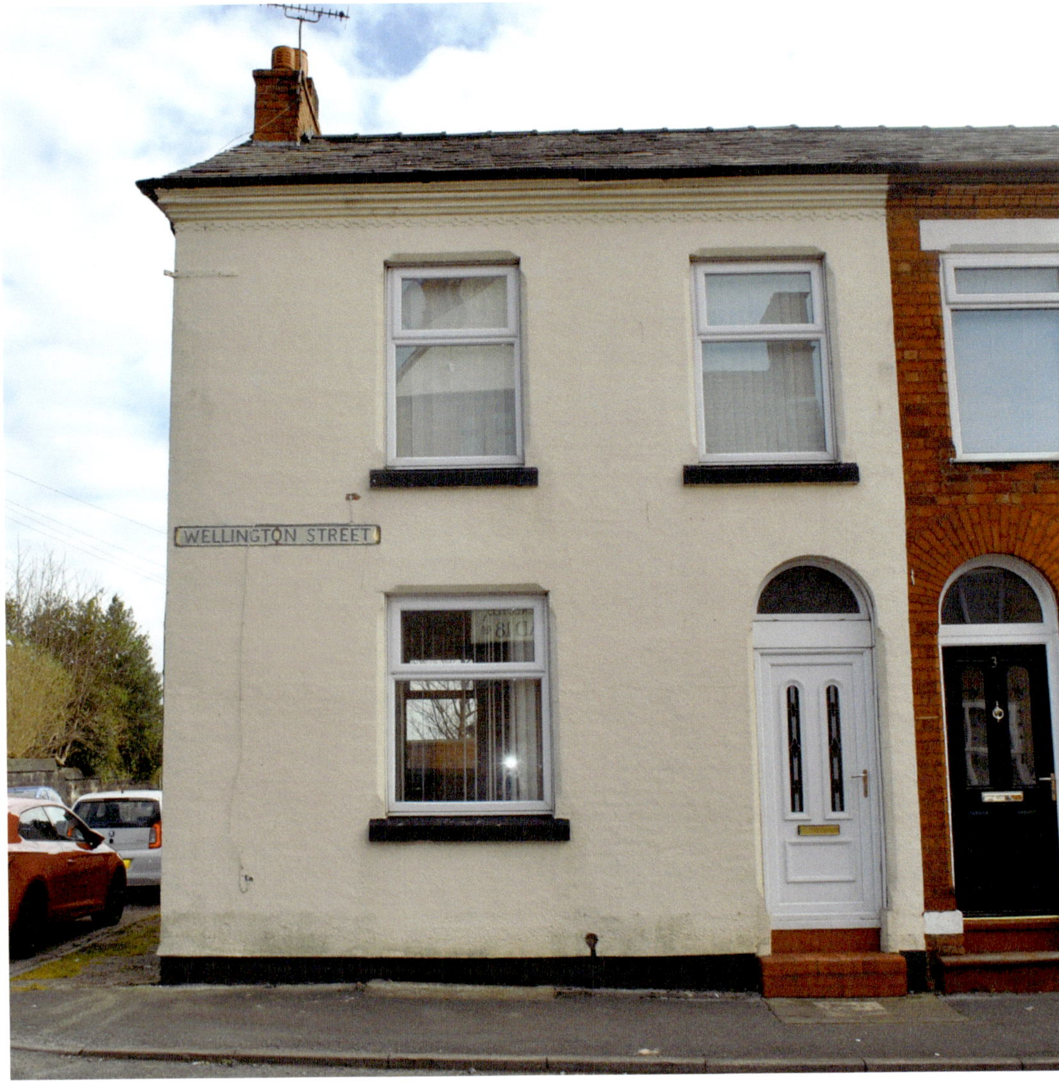

No. 1 Wellington Street, Castle. (Source: author)

and his wife died five years later in January 1941. Their grave can be found in Knutsford Cemetery on Tabley Hill Lane. Frank expanded the business from two to eight bakers and, in 1937, began considering further expansion. There was an old, established bakery business in Warrington Road, Northwich, owned and built up by Alfred Middleton. Roberts purchased the bakery, and they continued with the new bakery under its original name but remained at the head office, Nos 24–26 Station Road, Lostock.

When output grew to three times normal levels during the war, it was decided that the Warrington Road site was not large enough. Frank Roberts agreed that the two bakeries should be united in a purpose-built one, and what they needed was a site in open country with clean, fresh air and hygienic surroundings. Frank's sons, Alan and Bernard, had joined the firm, and David joined later after leaving school. Alan Roberts had spent two years at Manchester School of Technology on a £250 scholarship studying bakery. The war was still

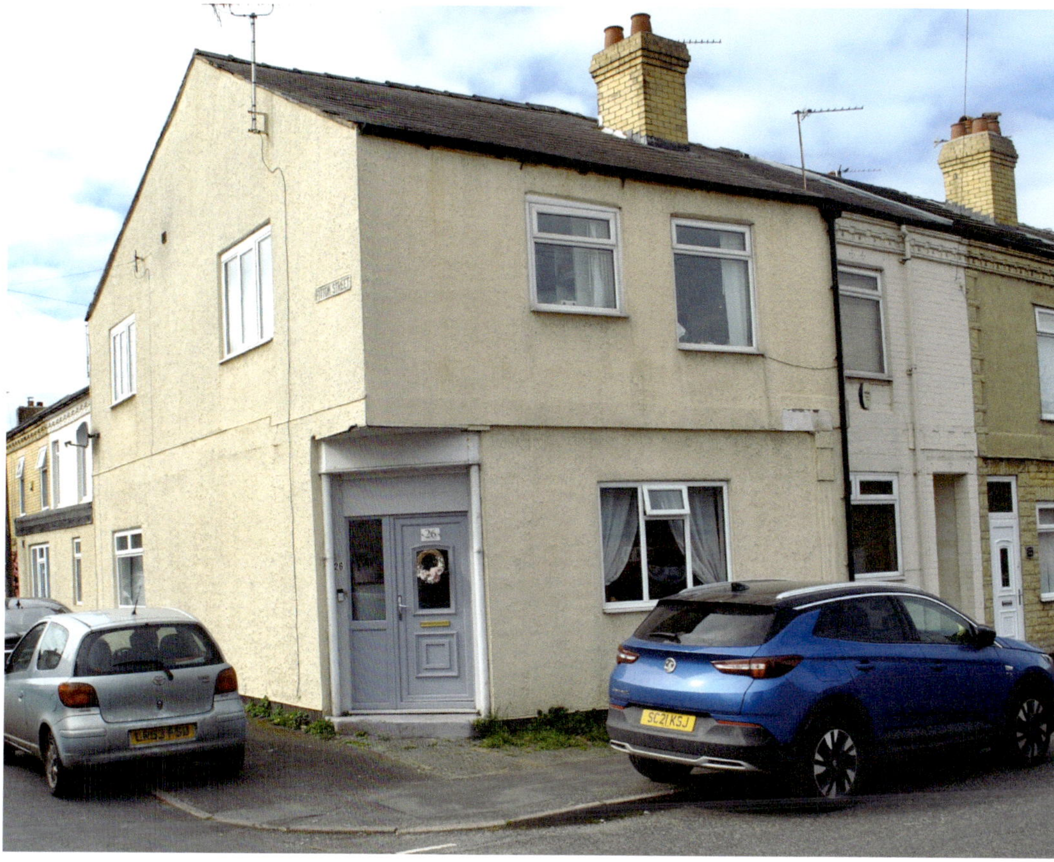

Nos 24–26 Station Road, Lostock. (Source: author)

ongoing, and he joined the RAF and, after training in Canada, won his wings. In the meantime, work started on the new bakery. On demob, Alan returned to the family business.

A site was chosen, and in 1951 Frank Roberts received his building licence for a 2.5-acre site on the Northwich Bypass, opposite the new primary school. In 1952, Frank Roberts pressed the master switch and set in motion his new bakery in School Road, Rudheath. His son Alan Roberts oversaw the new bakery night shift that produced the first loaves on the new premises. The bakery was the most modern in Cheshire, and the two companies, Roberts (Lostock) Ltd and Middleton's Bakery, were brought together under one name, Frank Roberts and Sons Ltd, with, of course, the same management. Alan was starting to play a more important role and would soon run the business. Bernard oversaw the grocery side of the company. At about this time, the bakery's name was changed to the Red Rose Bakery.

Frank Roberts took the business onwards and upwards. As well as the Red Rose Bakery and Frank Roberts and Son's grocers and provision merchants, they also owned Price's Stores at Hartford.

On 5 May 1954, when he was just fifty-four years old, he had attended a meeting of the Mid Cheshire Education Executive at Northwich. Frank Roberts left early to travel to Manchester with family members and business associates. They were to visit the Grocery Exhibition at Belle Vue. Three cars were used for the trip, two driven by his sons, Alan and Bernard. On returning from Manchester, his vehicle was involved in a head-on crash with a car containing

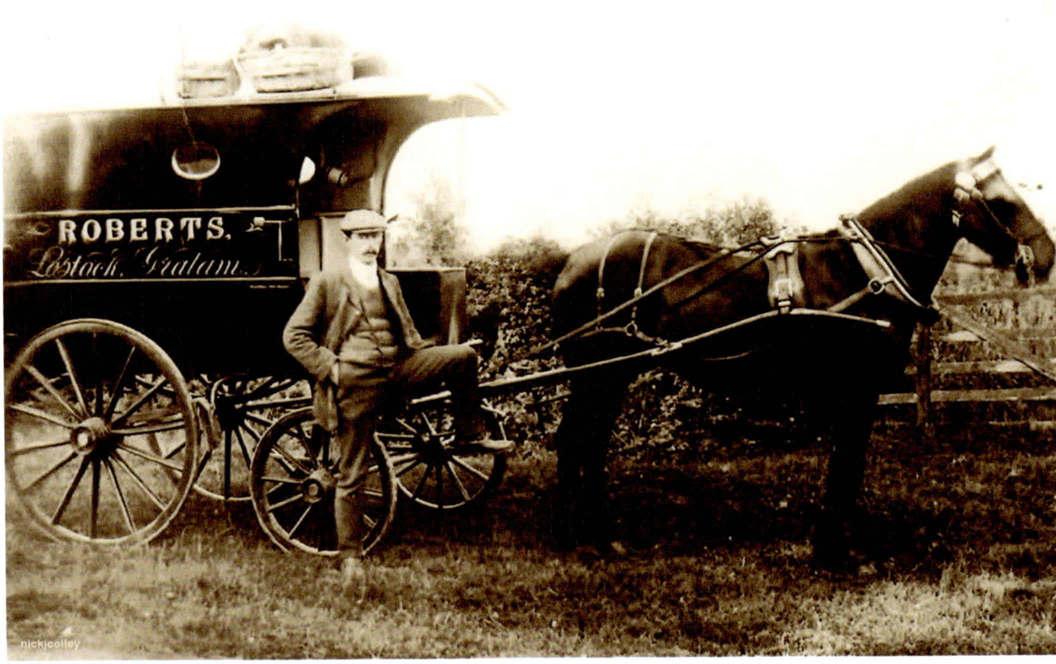

An early Roberts delivery van.

people from Macclesfield travelling in the opposite direction on Manchester Road, near the Smoker Inn. Frank, his wife and his youngest son, David, were taken to Altrincham General Hospital, where, sadly, Frank died.

One of the people in the other car also died in the crash. Frank's wife, Jennie, and son David recovered. Jennie died in 1959 whilst living at No. 65 Westfield Drive, Knutsford.

Alan Roberts took the helm at the bakery after his father's death, as it continued to grow with the name Frank Roberts and Sons Ltd. He served as the company's chairman and managing director for thirty-two years. In 1951, he had moved to Knutsford after marrying his wife, Muriel; later, he became an urban district councillor. By the 1960s, the company was producing 90,000 loaves a week and had a fleet of fifty vehicles to transport them. In 1986, he had suffered a severe stroke and stood down from the business. By this point he was married to his new wife, Helen. They moved to the United States, first settling in Illinois before moving to New Mexico, where Alan died in 2004 at the age of seventy-nine. A memorial service was held at St John's Church, Lostock, on Friday 16 July.

Already working for the company since 1976, the new generation consisted of Alan's son, Mike, Bernard's daughter, Julia, and, in 1984, David's daughter, Lindsay. The bakery continued to expand, remaining a family concern. In 1988, Little Treats Bakery was added, baking and decorating delicious gingerbread and iced treats. In 2000, a vast cooling tower was built which became another iconic building. Vehicles held at the traffic lights can now watch the bread going around and around within the expansive glass windows, with the aroma of freshly loaves bread wafting out.

A fire at the bakery in 2023 caused significant operational disruption. An article in the *Northwich Guardian* reported on Monday 6 October 2025 that a notice of intention to appoint administrators was issued.

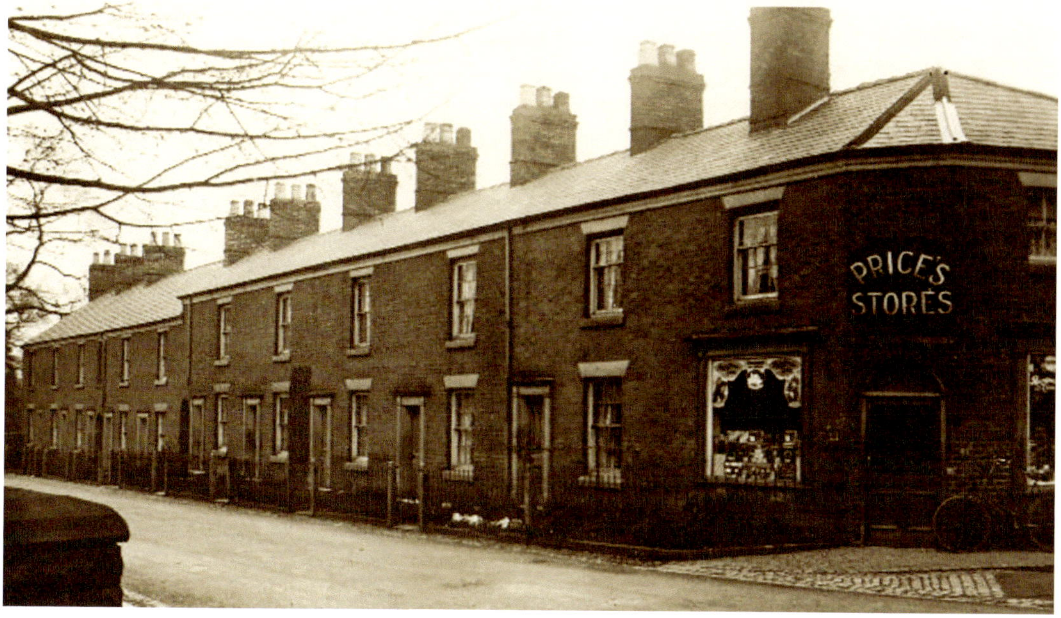

Price's Stores, Hartford.

When local family firms join multinationals and are acquired or sold off, firms like Broadhurst and ICI disappear or lose their distinctive identities; Frank Roberts and Sons Ltd has remained a family-owned firm. Professional and managerial expertise has been introduced into senior management. Small shops and supermarket shelves feature superior-quality products bearing the name Roberts Bakery. So, what Robert Roberts started in his little shop at No. 1 Wellington Street, Castle, is now a multinational, highly respected business, still based in Northwich and under the control of his descendants. The company also contributes significantly to the local community and charitable organisations.

Hopefully, the trials and tribulations caused by the recent fire will resolve and allow the company to continue serving customers in Cheshire and elsewhere. Having said that Roberts Bakery was a family concern, but after the serious fire this had to end as the company went into administration. Fortunately, there was an investment company interested and it would appear that the business will continue as Frank Roberts Bakery with most of the staff for the foreseeable future. (Source: Roberts and author)

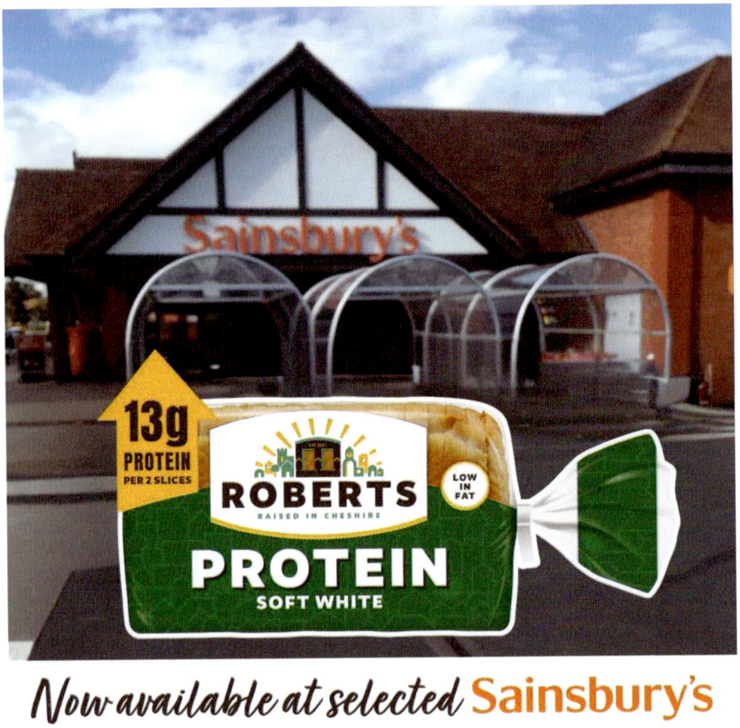

Roberts Bakery advert.

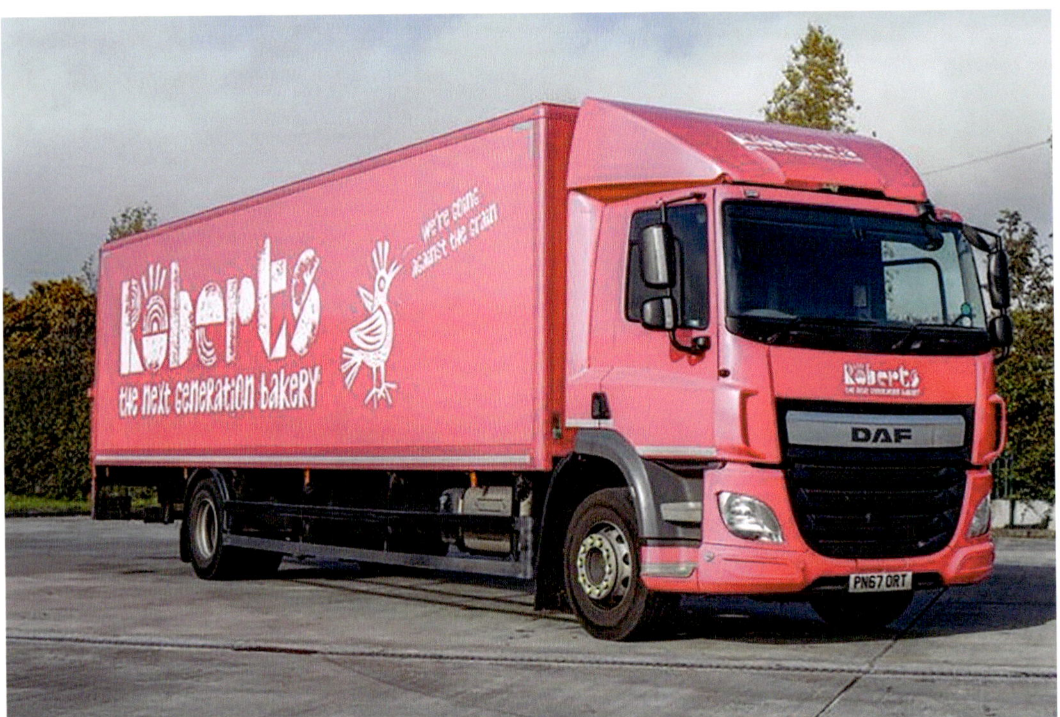

Roberts Bakery van.

THE SHORT-LIVED YET IMPORTANT MILL INDUSTRY IN NORTHWICH

William Cockshott was an entrepreneur born in Bolton in 1753 who, due to the rivers Weaver and Dane, took a shine to Northwich as a potential location for mills and, in 1780, built a cotton mill in the centre of Northwich on the River Weaver. It was recorded in the diary of the parish church of Witton that there was extreme excitement in Northwich because of the potential economic industrial expansion in this area. In April 1780, Cockshott requested permission from the Weaver Navigation Committee to use wastewater from the existing Northwich weir. This enabled the manufacture of cotton, and the mill was subsequently built.

In 1781, Daniel Whittaker began with a tentative foot in the water by considering Acton Bridge, just a couple of miles from Northwich, as a location for a mill. Prior to this, Macclesfield and Congleton were the main silk mill centres in Cheshire.

It was noted in the late 1700s that Northwich was to become one of the pioneering mill towns, driven by investment in this and other locations such as Holywell, Manchester and East Cheshire. In addition, recent inventions to mechanise mills by Richard Arkwright, who lived from 1732 to 1792, were changing the face of 'modern' milling. Arkwright developed a simple yet clever piece of machinery that replaced the work of human hands. The water frame (also known as the spinning frame) enabled the spinning of cotton yarn far more quickly and in greater quantities than ever before. These inventions enabled wealthy mill owners to exploit the machines by investing profits into existing mills, reducing the workforce and increasing productivity.

In 1782, a gentleman named Peter Drinkwater was a wealthy and successful cotton manufacturer and merchant from Whalley, Lancashire. He owned the very first cotton Mill in Manchester, powered by a steam engine; it was only the tenth such mill in the world. Construction of the four-storey Piccadilly Mill began in 1789, and by 1 May 1791, the 8-hp Boulton and Watt engine had been installed and was operational. During the 1790s, the mill employed around 500 workers.

Peter Drinkwater was looking for investment opportunities. He was already a fustian manufacturer in Bolton and Manchester, and he wanted to expand into cotton manufacture by purchasing the Cockshott Mill just two years after its erection. He was quoted as saying, 'a situation on the River Weaver which, for water and hands, cannot be exceeded by any in the kingdom'.

In 1783, Drinkwater decided to upgrade his newly acquired property by improving the water flow to provide the requisite waterpower. To do this would require a new weir to be

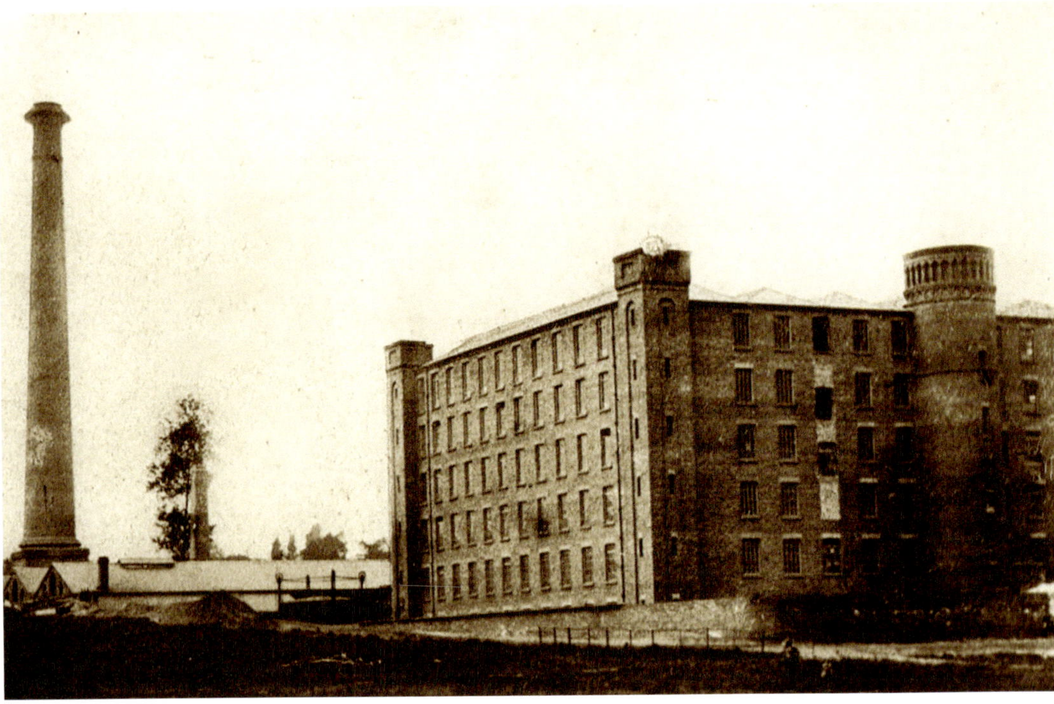

Over Mill, Winsford.

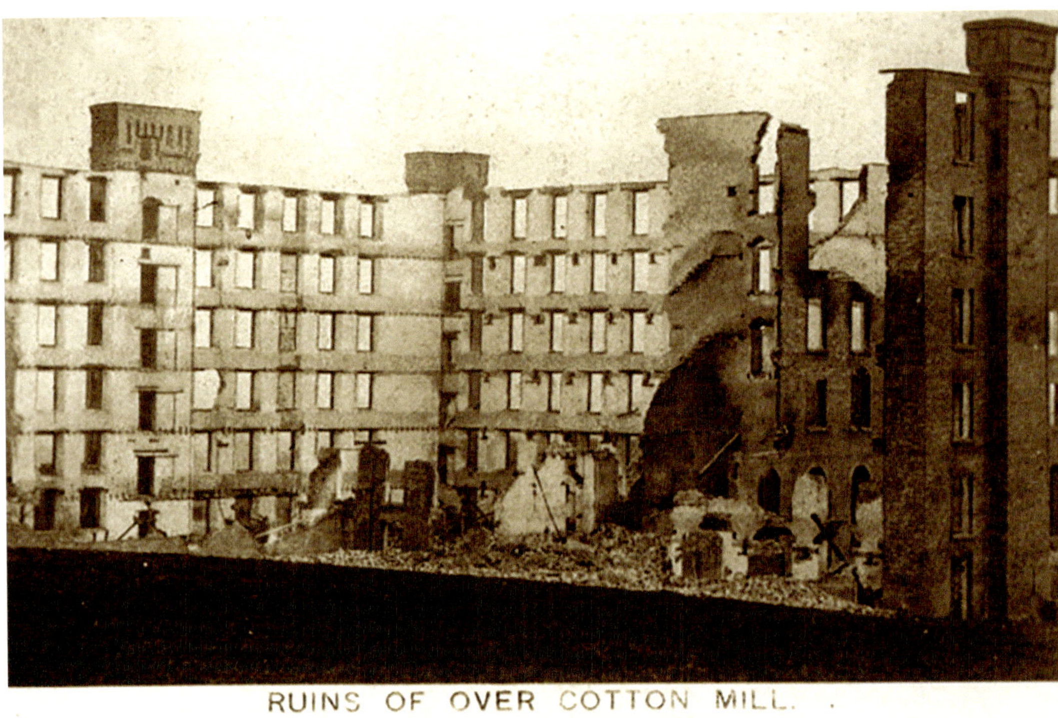

Over Mill burnt out.

constructed across the River Dane just before it joined the Weaver in the centre of the town. In effect, this diverted water into a canal running from Baron's Croft Saltworks to the cotton works at Barons Quay.

In 1797, plans were afoot to improve aspects of Witton Brook, with knock-on consequences for the head of water at Northwich weir. A lock sank, causing extensive repairs, during which the lack of water to the mill led to Mr Drinkwater being awarded £1,000 in compensation (equivalent to £192,680 today).

In February 1799, a newspaper report stated that the extensive cotton mills in Northwich, owned by Peter Drinkwater, had been destroyed by fire.

Interestingly, in 1810, the Baron Croft works were shown as for sale and included an excellent-quality stone race to a waterwheel with great power, at a leasehold plot of land called 'the cotton works'. The wheel power had been used for the raising of brine since 1803, perhaps as a result of the fire of 1799, which appeared to call a halt to cotton mills in Northwich.

Later, nearby Winsford had a cotton mill, but it operated only briefly. However, we can still use the photographs and story from that one.

In 1869, a large cotton spinning and doubling mill was built by Messrs Abraham Haigh and Sons on the High Street side of St George's Road in Winsford. It was so big it stretched almost to what would become Well Street, which was given the name in tribute to the well that was situated there and was used to power the mill's machinery. The head of the family was Mr James Haigh; in 1860, he purchased Darnhall Hall and renovated it.

New streets were planned to house the workers from the mill. Unfortunately, there was no time to complete that project in full, although roads were built and cotton workers from Lancashire were brought over and housed. As for Winsford, there were plenty of women to

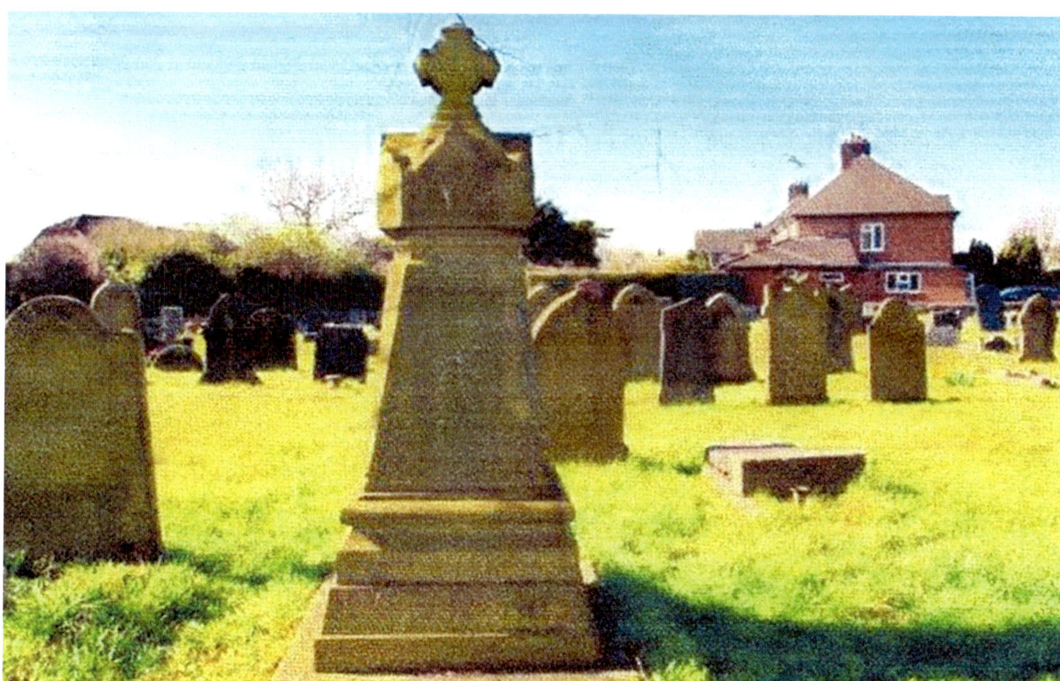

Monument to the Over Mill dead.

work at the mill. A law had just been passed to prevent women from working in the mines. The mill employed 300 workers and disaster struck at 5 p.m. on Tuesday 27 October 1874, just five years after opening, when a fire broke out in the spinning room. The subsequent finding at the inquest was that friction had caused a spark to ignite nearby cotton waste. The fire spread rapidly through the mill, trapping many workers. Harriet Whitehurst and her three-month-old baby died when she jumped from the fourth floor after trying to drop the baby into a water tank, but her thirteen-year-old daughter, Margaret, was successful at escaping.

In all, eight people died in the inferno. Poor James Haigh was not very lucky financially. The week before the fire, he was negotiating the sale of the mill, and it was temporarily uninsured, which drove him into bankruptcy. The remains of the main mill building were demolished, but the chimney and boiler house were saved. The chimney remained in situ until 1904, when it was demolished. Some of the bricks were used to build the nearby Upper and Lower Haigh Streets, which were named in tribute to the Haigh family. The people of Winsford paid for a monument in the new church of St John's and erected it over the single grave containing the eight who died. All the names are engraved upon it. This fire put an end to Winsford's hopes of being a cotton town.

HANLEY'S FLOUR MILL, NORTHWICH

Hanley's Flour Mill and warehouse were situated just before the Dane Bridge in Northwich. This large flour mill was built in the 1800s and stood firm for years until the dreaded subsidence began. It suffered spectacularly, as shown in these first two images, dated to the late 1800s. The last one dates to the early 1900s.

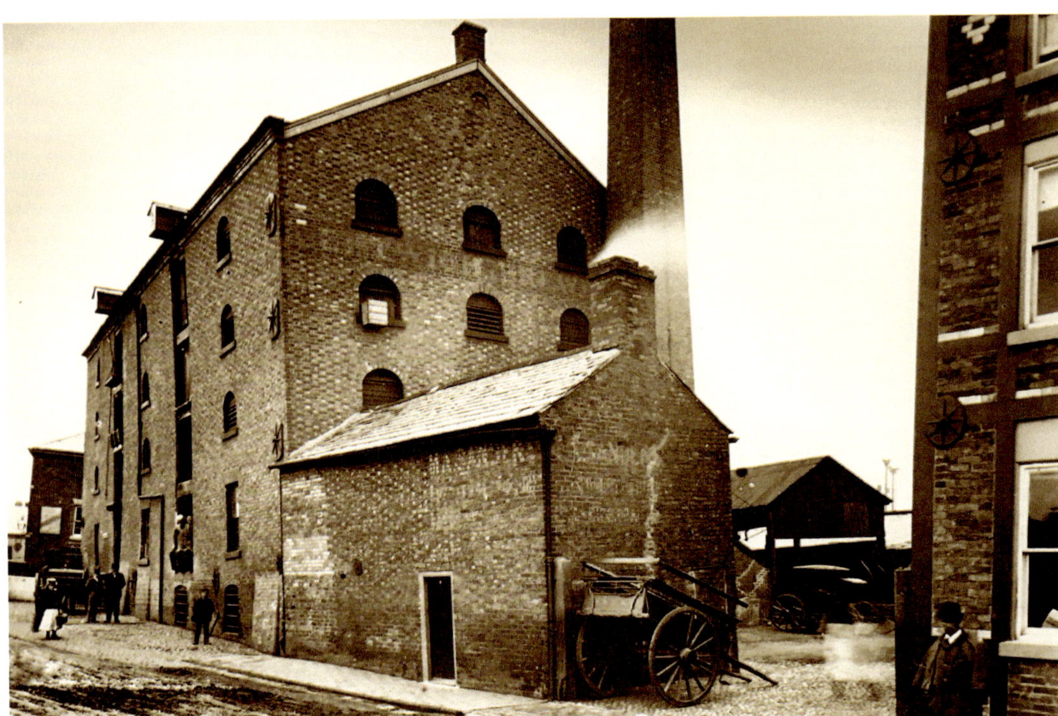

Above and next page: Hanley's Flour Mill, Northwich, 1891.

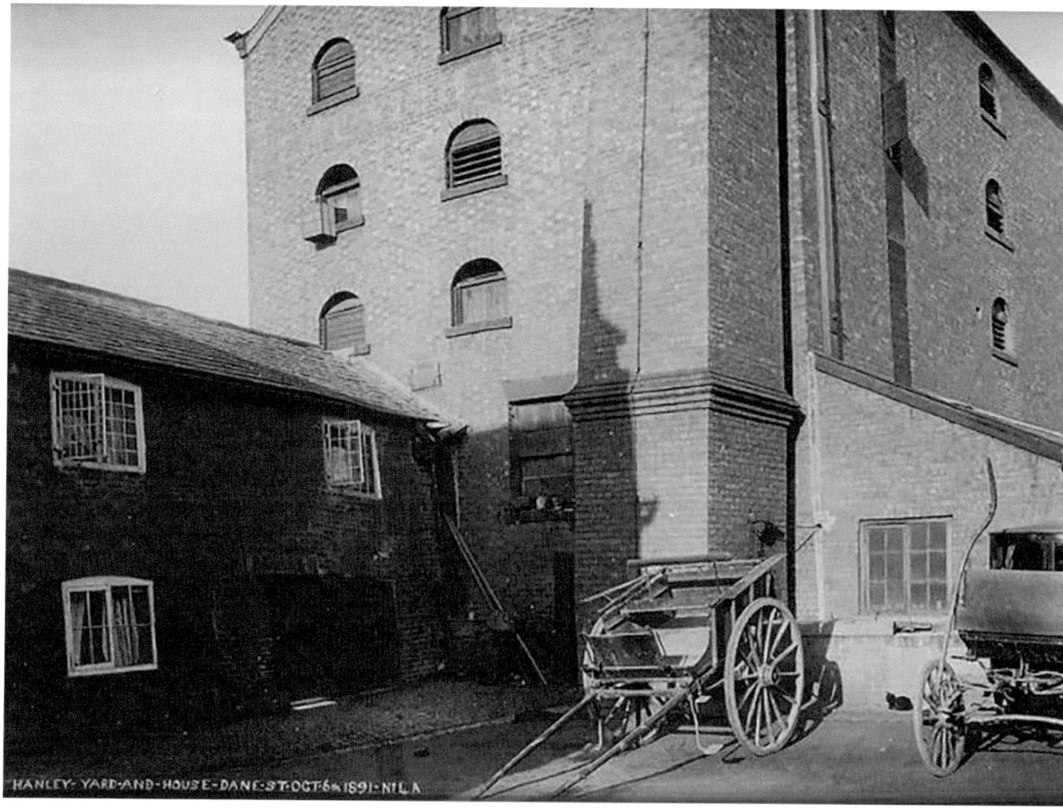
HANLEY-YARD-AND-HOUSE-DANE-ST-OCT-6th 1891-NILA

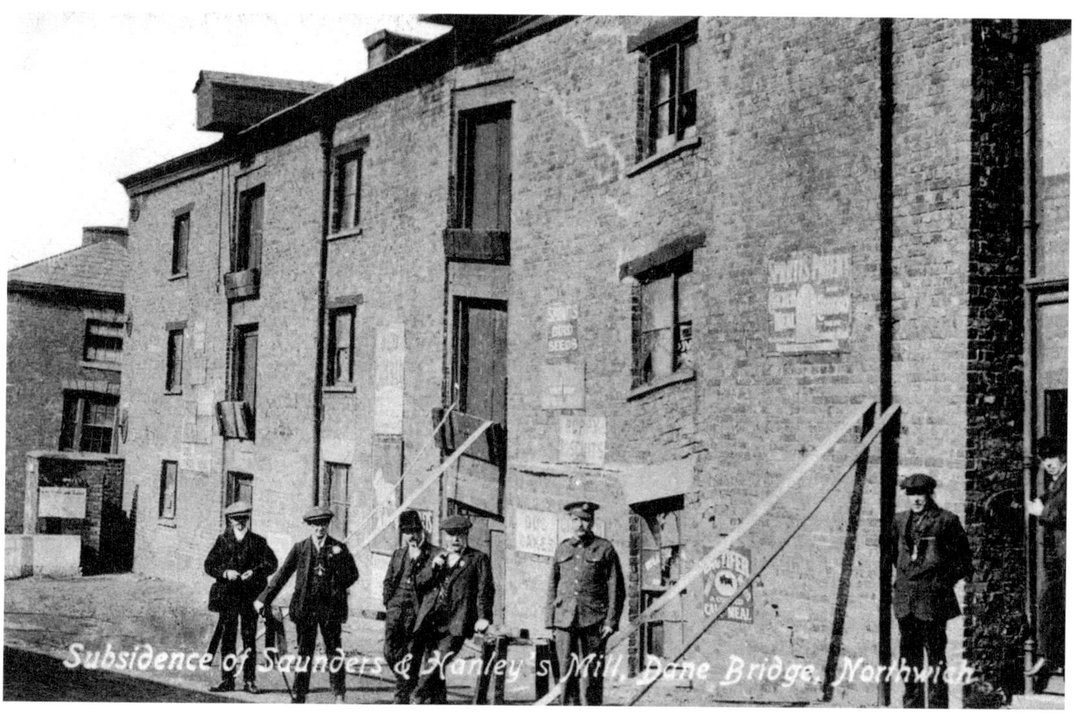
Subsidence of Saunders & Hanley's Mill, Dane Bridge, Northwich

JOSEPH PARKS & SON STEELWORKS

The company was formed in 1861 by Joseph Parks Sr and initially was engaged in light engineering works. They made tools and vessels for the salt and engineering companies. In 1881, Joseph Parks lived at Croft House, No. 83 Manchester Road, Northwich, and was a boiler maker.

A big contract they were engaged in in January 1872 was a large new salt pan at the Verdin mine in Marston. These pans were massive and made from heavy steel. Whilst trying to insert a prop, the pan began to sway under its weight and fell to the ground, where three men were working. Two of them were the Holland brothers, William and Joseph. Joseph was crushed to death, and his brother was injured. The third man, Samuel Hitchen, was severely injured, and another man sustained a broken leg.

The firm was not always successful. They tendered for the construction of the two Northwich swing bridges built in the 1890s, but lost out to another company, Andrew Handyside Ltd of Derby. The company later succeeded in tendering and being accepted for the construction of the Acton Swing Bridge and the Sutton Weaver Swing Bridge. They secured the contract to provide the reinforced steel for a water tower at Warbreck, Blackpool, for the Fylde Water Board. It was the largest such building in Great Britain at the time.

By 1901, Joseph's sons, Joseph and John, were also described as boiler makers. Around 1919, the company gained a new leader; Harold Bentley Denton took over as chairman and managing director. The name remained the same – Joseph Parks and Son – but under Mr Denton, it became a major steel fabrication establishment of worldwide reputation.

But what of this man who had taken the helm and turned Northwich into a mecca for steel fabrication and erection? Harold Bentley Denton was born in Colchester, Essex, in 1884 and was listed as a major in the Royal Air Force (Royal Flying Corps) in the First World War. He was awarded the OBE (Military Division) in 1919 for his war service. He started his engineering career in Colchester with a firm of boiler makers and steam locomotive builders.

It was during his time in Manchester that his military career began, as he joined the Lancashire Volunteer Battalion of the Royal Fusiliers. At the outbreak of the First World War, he was mobilised with the Territorial Army, then the Royal Engineers, and finally the Royal Flying Corps, gaining the rank of major. Upon demobilisation, he resumed his employment with Joseph Parks Steelworks, now also known as Wadebrook Steelworks, and travelled widely on

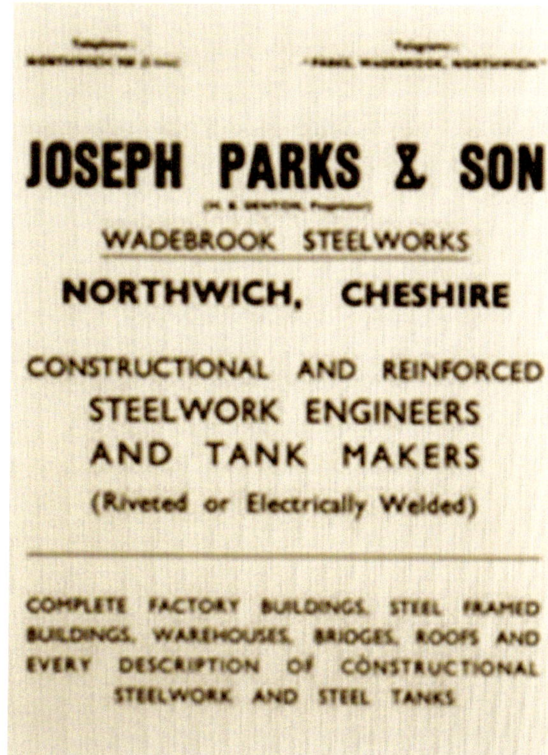

Joseph Parks & Son advert.
(Source: John Quigley)

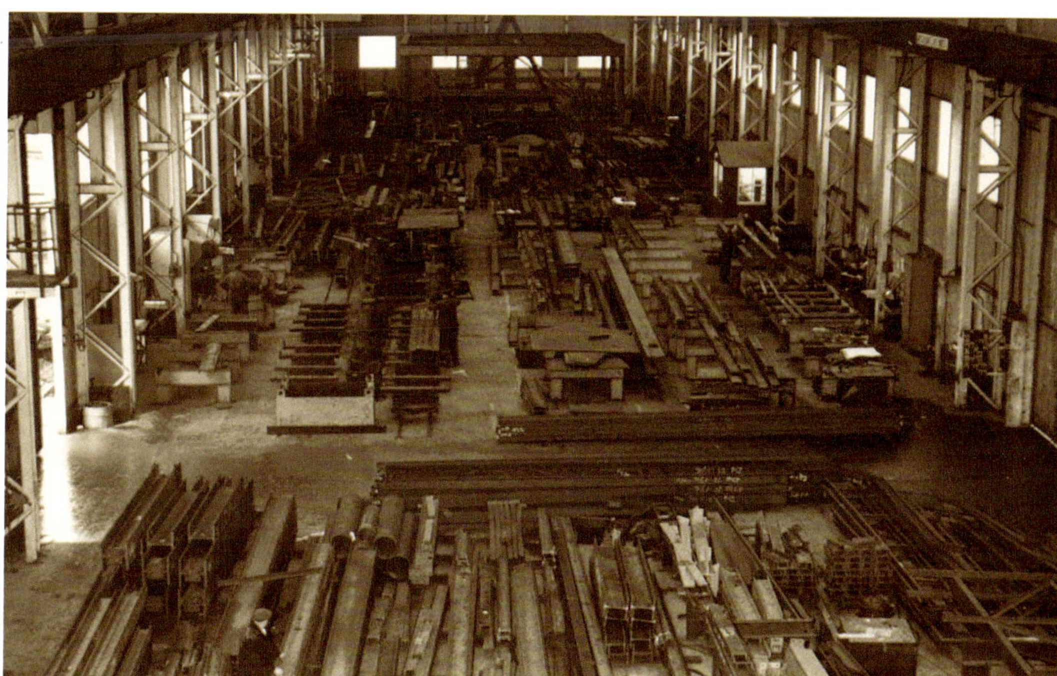

Template shop at Joseph Parks & Son.

behalf of the company. During his time in Northwich, he became an executive of the British Constructional Steelwork Association. He was a founder member of the Northwich Branch of the Royal British Legion. At the start of the Second World War, he rallied service veterans into the Local Defence Volunteers, and when this became the Home Guard, he was given command of it with the rank of Lieutenant-Colonel. In his younger days, he played in goal for Colchester FC, but his first love was cricket. While living in Davenham, he played cricket for the village team, serving as both a player and a chairman.

During his time at the helm of Joseph Parks, a few of their contracts were as follows. During the Second World War, they were one of the contractors building the Mulberry Harbours which would be towed to Arromanches on the French coast in preparation for D-Day. The company worked on the steel buildings at Winnington Works, Lostock Works and later Wallerscote Works. The company built the Sutton Weaver Swing Bridge at Frodsham in 1926, followed by the Acton Swing Bridge at Acton Bridge in 1933 (the last one designed by John Arthur Saner). They built the stand at Port Vale FC in Hanley.

H. B. Denton's son, Ronald Bentley Denton, would take over from him on his retirement on ill health grounds in 1958. At the time of his retirement, Joseph Parks & Son were working in Abu Dhabi in the Persian Gulf, in India, and in Southern Rhodesia.

They worked on the Piccadilly Hotel in London and many other contracts at home and abroad. In 1962, Harold Denton died at his home, Overdale, in Sandiway.

Not to be beaten by his father's wartime record, Ronald was a war hero. He was a Lieutenant-Colonel and the holder of a Military Cross and Bar; he had also been mentioned in dispatches. The company continued to grow. They provided the steel and the steel fixing at the Northwich Victoria Memorial Hall, later better known locally as the much-loved 'Morgue'. In 1975, the company constructed five buildings and a bridge at a Brazilian shipyard. Work continued under Ronald Denton's leadership. The end came in 1986, when the company closed, and the land became Northwich Retail Park, housing shops such as B&Q, Argos, Currys, PC World, and others. The company may be no more, but the steelworks constructed there can still be seen around Britain and the world.

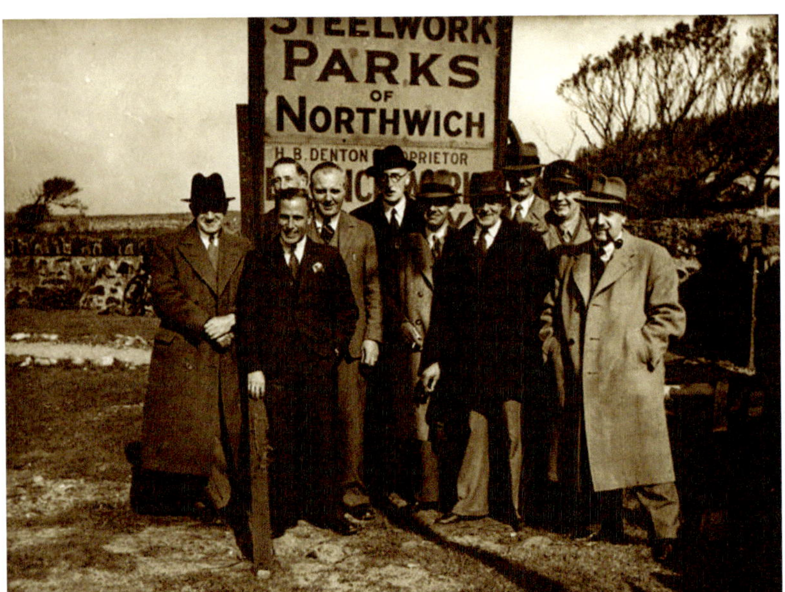

Parks' management team.

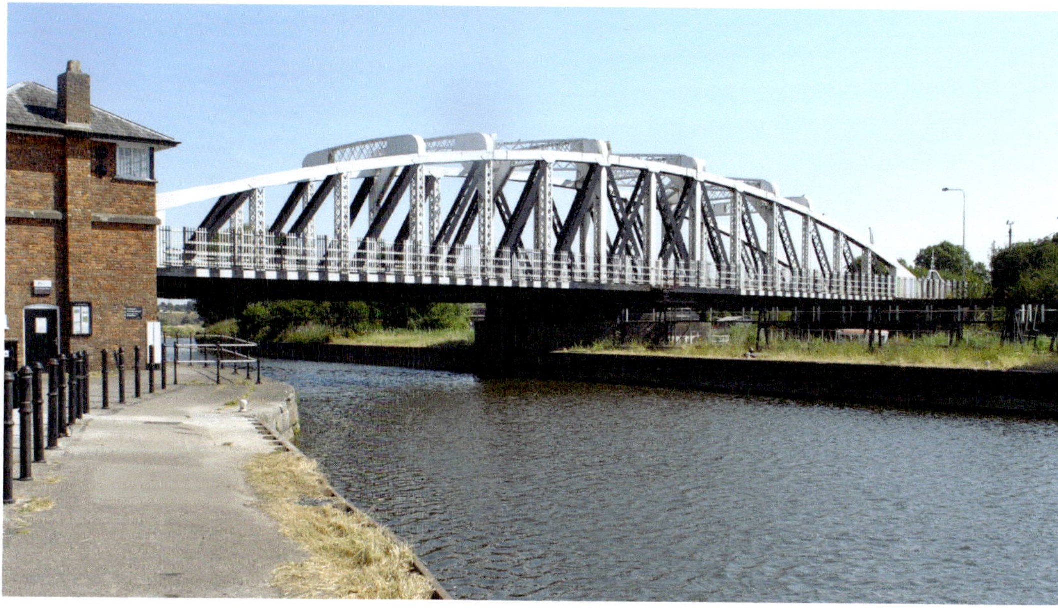

Acton Swing Bridge. (Source: author)

REDFERN'S RUBBER WORKS LTD

The initial Redfern's company was founded by Wilfred Redfern in 1900 to supply cycle tyres and pedal rubbers, along with other items for the cycle trade. Initially, they worked from a dwelling house, but Wilfred was later joined by his brother Thomas, and they moved to larger premises in Clarendon Street, Hyde. As well as supplying cycle parts, they registered the Non-Slipping Silent Heel Company Ltd in 1905 with £80,000 and changed the name to Redfern's Rubber Works Ltd. The company continued to go from strength to strength, and the works were subsequently extended. Mr Arnold Redfern was appointed in 1911 to open the first branch depot at No. 10 Gresham Street, London. Diplomas and medals were won at Liege (1905), London (1906), Milan (1906) and Turin (1911). In 1912, it was decided to manufacture cycle tyres, tubes and solid tyres for commercial vehicles.

The business grew and completed government contracts during the First World War. Planning for the end of the war, they opened further branches in Glasgow, Bristol and Leeds. In early 1920, the company's capital was £200,000 (equivalent to £11,423,530 in 2026). Then came the great slump of 1920–22, and in common with the whole of British commerce, the company suffered. Unprofitable departments were shut down, and the Glasgow and Bristol depots were closed, but the company redoubled its efforts at home and abroad.

A factory was purchased at Wincham near Northwich, and production of tennis shoes and felt slippers with rubber soles commenced there. Mr R. H. Boulton from Rossendale was the manager of the tennis shoe factory, and he remained in that position until it closed in 1932. He Lived at 'Rossendale', Chester Road, Hartford. The house's name may have been taken from his old hometown, where he died in 1937.

Experiments were made in the laboratory and in the works to find new lines for manufacture to take the place of the lost trade. Emerging from this research work were departments for the manufacture of 'Tufthide' soles and heels, 'Ebonite' goods for the wireless and electrical trades, advertising mats and household rubbers, as well as rubber flooring and interlocking rubber tiles.

In 1924, Mr T. C. Redfern retired and Mr J. Arthur Redfern was appointed works managing director to fill the vacancy.

On 22 October 1926, HRH Princess Helena Victoria visited the works and graciously accepted a gift of rubber table mats as a souvenir of the occasion. By then, the company had grown and progressively broadened its operations. From being solely manufacturers of rubber heels and soles, the firm was by then established as general rubber manufacturers. They employed hundreds of workers at their Hyde and Wincham factories, as well as a large number of salespeople and depot staff in other parts of the country.

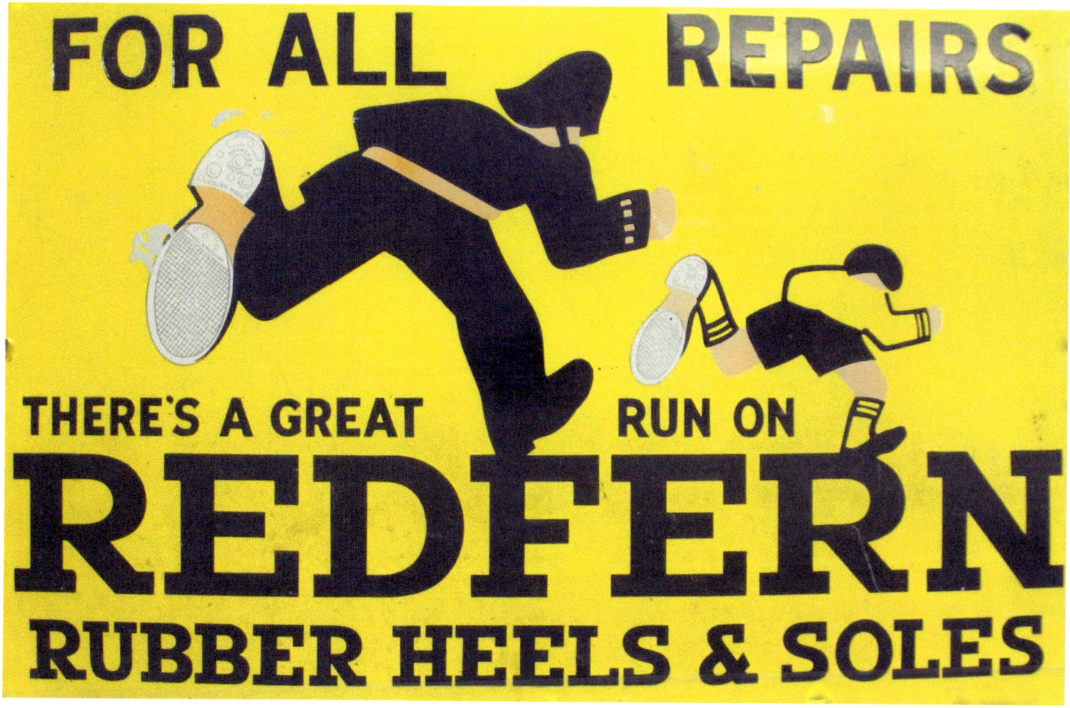

Redfern's advert.

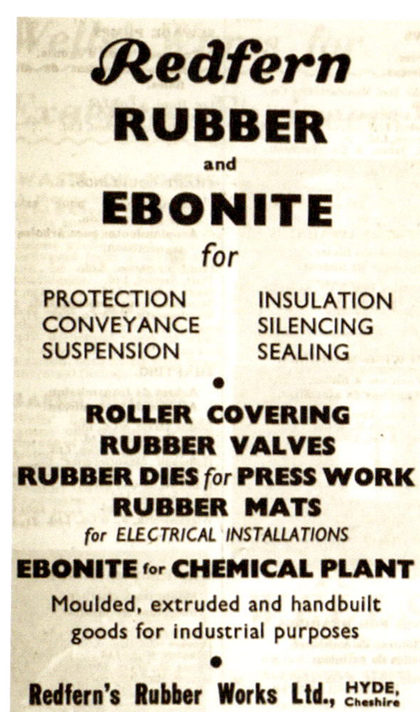

Redfern's advert.

ACTON BRIDGE AND ITS LONG-LOST INDUSTRY

The old stone bridge led to the turn bridge and continues along the main road towards Bartington. Now it leads across the new cut in the river to the island. The latest swing bridge was opened on 19 August 1933. The river splits into two here, with one course navigable via a swing bridge and the other, once with a sluice, crossed by the stone bridge that is still there. This image overleaf clearly shows the old stone bridge and the Acton Swing Bridge. The river is split, leaving an island in the centre. Looking to the left, you will come to the row of cottages, originally homes for the workers on the site. Further down is the Riverside Inn, once an abattoir, and then continuing for some distance towards Weaverham.

There was a sawmill, a zinc works, manure works, bone mills, a forge and a saltpetre works. All were helped by the waterwheel situated near the sluice on the river. There was also a packet boat service from the wharves and warehouses.

The Acton area was described by George Ormerod (1785–1873) in his *History of Cheshire* as:

> A district consisting of fine meadow ground sloping to the banks of the Weever and not destitute of pleasing undulations of surface of fine timber, which here, receiving protection from the sea breezes. Begins to attain its wonted luxuriency where deer range from the forest to the banks of the Weever.

When I was working on the farm that was on the other side of the River Weaver and opposite the Rheingold Restaurant, now the Riverside Inn, my boss told me that if I dug into the big bank in the car park, what would come out would be white, as it was once a boneyard and abattoir.

I mentioned this at the Riverside Inn and no one was aware. What they also weren't aware of was that this was a heavily industrialised location. Hard to believe now, but over the years, the site was home to a zinc works, a mill, and a manufacturer of gunpowder and fertiliser from animal products. Its last title was the Weaver Refining Company.

Apart from the pub, nothing is left of what was a hive of heavy and smelly industry. However, considerable material is available on this large industrial factory situated in the centre of Cheshire, and the website by John Birchall provides much helpful information. The factory was owned by his grandfather, Edward Hindley. I thank John for this hard work; a small example is used here.

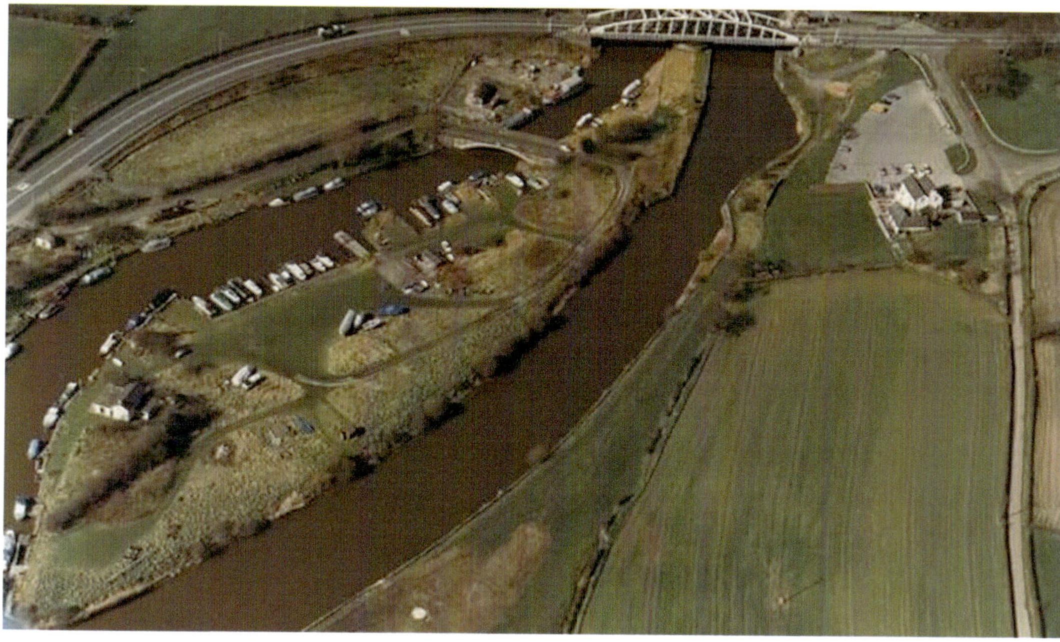

Approximate position of the works further towards Weaverham. (Source: author)

As time went by, in addition to manufacturing zinc, dead cows and bones were delivered from Acton Bridge station and ground to dust to make fertiliser. By 1871, this proved to be quite lucrative, and zinc rolling gave way to specialising in the manufacture of gunpowder from crushed bone and saltpetre. The manufacture of saltpetre is a rather smelly occupation and involves the use of animal waste. Saltpetre requires nitre beds, which are created by mixing waste products such as urine, dark manure, and the contents of privies, cesspits, and drains. As this heap ripens in the sun, the saltpetre rises to the surface. Gunpowder is made using sulphuric acid, charcoal and potassium nitrate (saltpetre). The smell from this process was already unpleasant, but in 1871, the mill was known as the Manure Works. In 1882, the mill's power source was converted from water to steam. By then, the smell across Acton must have been truly toxic.

In 1905, it was reported in the *Northwich Guardian* that the Weaver Refining Company, located at the Riverside Inn, had taken over a horse slaughtering business. Kelly's Directory from 1902 to 1914 records the Weaver Refining Company, and in 1915, electricity came to the company. By 1916, this huge conglomerate in sleepy Cheshire had an office in Holborn, London. The site was also the company office block. On 7 May 1920, the company merged with the British Glues and Chemicals Company. The Acton Bridge site closed in 1923. Now, Acton Bridge smells nice again. (Source: John Redfern)

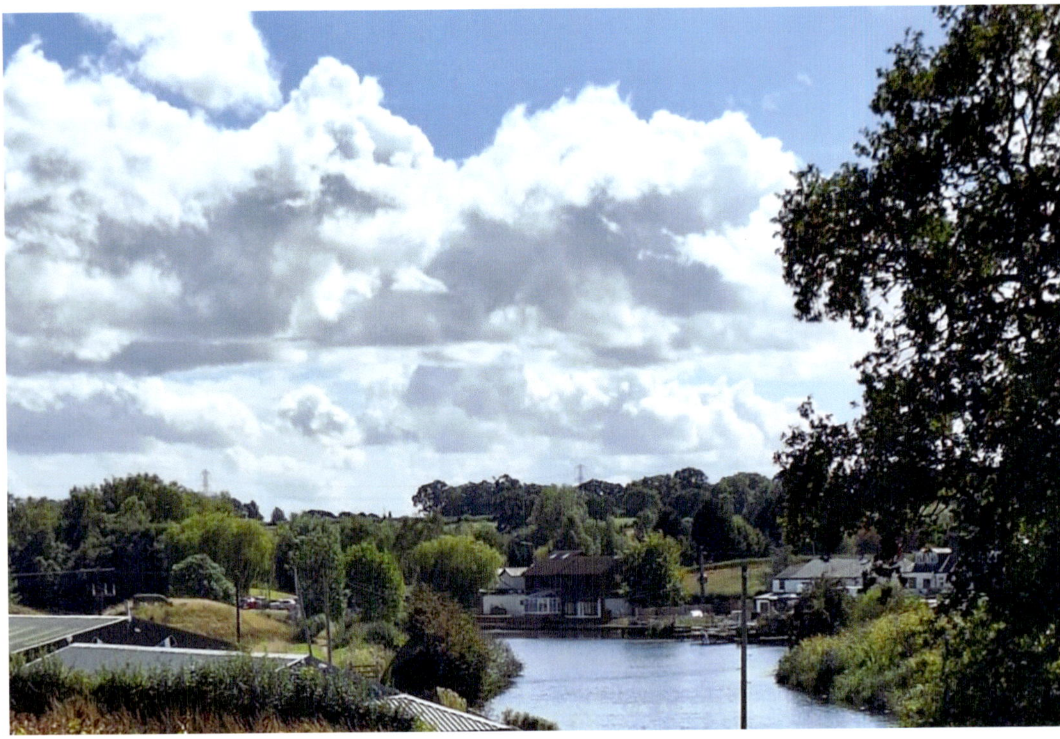

Continuation of the riverbank away from the abattoir.

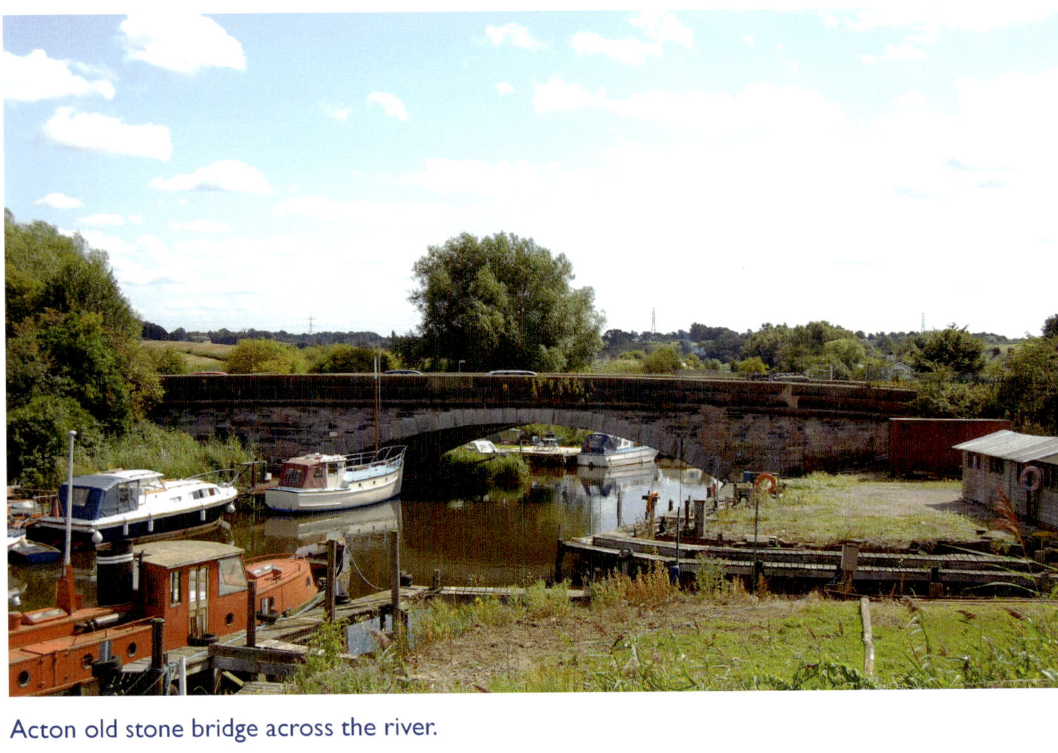

Acton old stone bridge across the river.

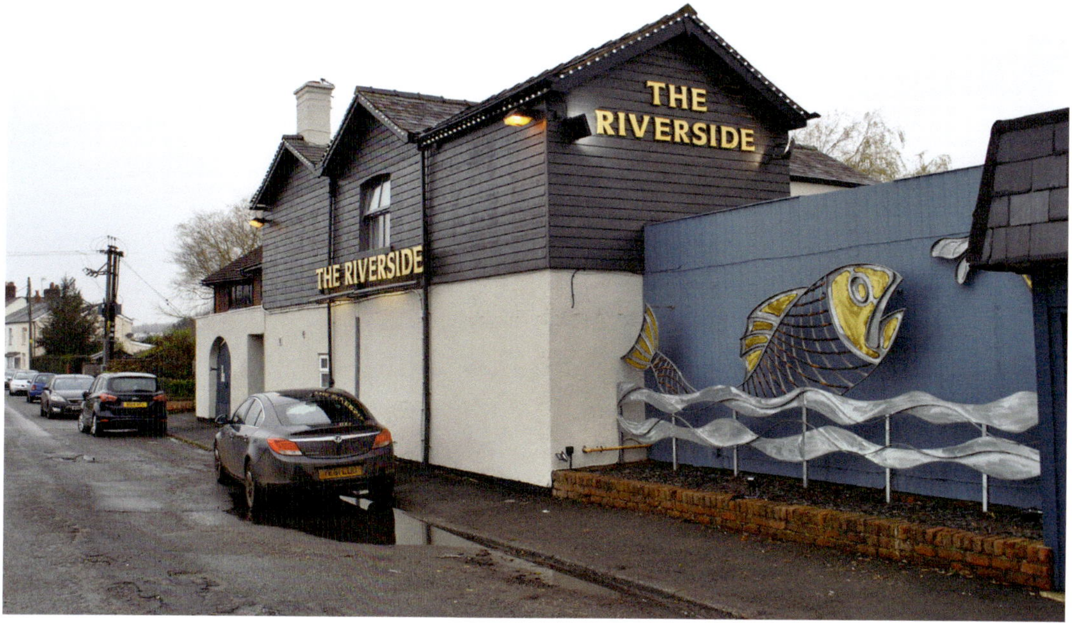

The Riverside pub.

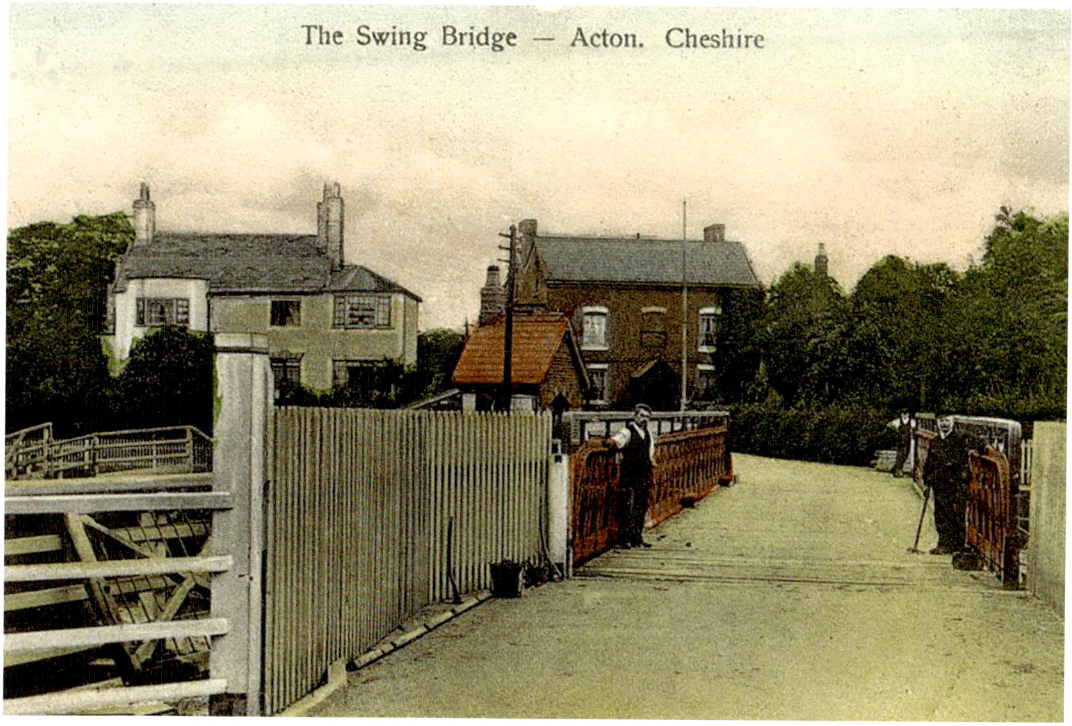

Acton Swing Bridge.

WINCHAM'S SERIOUS WAR WORK

Frank Whittle was born on 1 June 1907 in Coventry. His first attempts to join the RAF failed due to his height. In 1923, however, he was accepted as an apprentice, and in 1928, he qualified as a pilot officer. He had always been interested in engineering, and as an air cadet, he had written a thesis arguing that planes flying at high altitudes, where air resistance is much lower, could achieve greater range at higher speeds. This could not be achieved, he wrote, using piston engines and propellers, and he concluded that rocket propulsion would be required. At this stage, jet propulsion was not considered, and propellers were still needed. By October 1929, he considered installing a fan in the fuselage to generate a high-velocity airflow, thereby propelling the plane at high altitude. A piston engine would use too much fuel and take up too much storage space, so he thought of using a gas turbine. He put the proposal to the Air Ministry, and they turned it down; accordingly, he patented the idea himself. In 1935, Whittle secured financial backing, and, with the RAF's approval, Power Jets Ltd was formed.

It is worth noting that the Germans were also working on a jet engine. Hans von Ohain worked in conjunction with Heinkel and patented the use of a gas turbine for propulsion in 1935. Heinkel offered support to Ohain, suggesting that perhaps the RAF was slow to support Frank Whittle. In 1937, Heinkel had developed Ohain's ideas and conducted the first successful jet-engine test with the German jet plane, the Heinkel He 178, the world's first jet-powered aircraft, which flew in August 1939.

Power Jets Ltd began constructing a test engine in July 1936, but it proved inconclusive. Whittle concluded that a complete rebuild was required, but lacked the necessary finances. Protracted negotiations with the Air Ministry followed, and the project was secured in 1940. By April 1941, the engine was ready for tests. The company working on the early jet engine was Metropolitan-Vickers in Manchester. The war had begun, and a location was needed to test the jet engine.

Leslie Stubbs managed the New Cheshire Salt Works at Wincham, and his brother Albert Stubbs was an engineer with knowledge of the jet project. At his request, his brother agreed to provide some land and a building to carry out the tests. Security was strict, and the employees had to sign the Official Secrets Act and say nothing about this groundbreaking research. The engine's loud noise on the test bed left the locals wondering what was going on in the mysterious building known as F2 on the salt works' grounds.

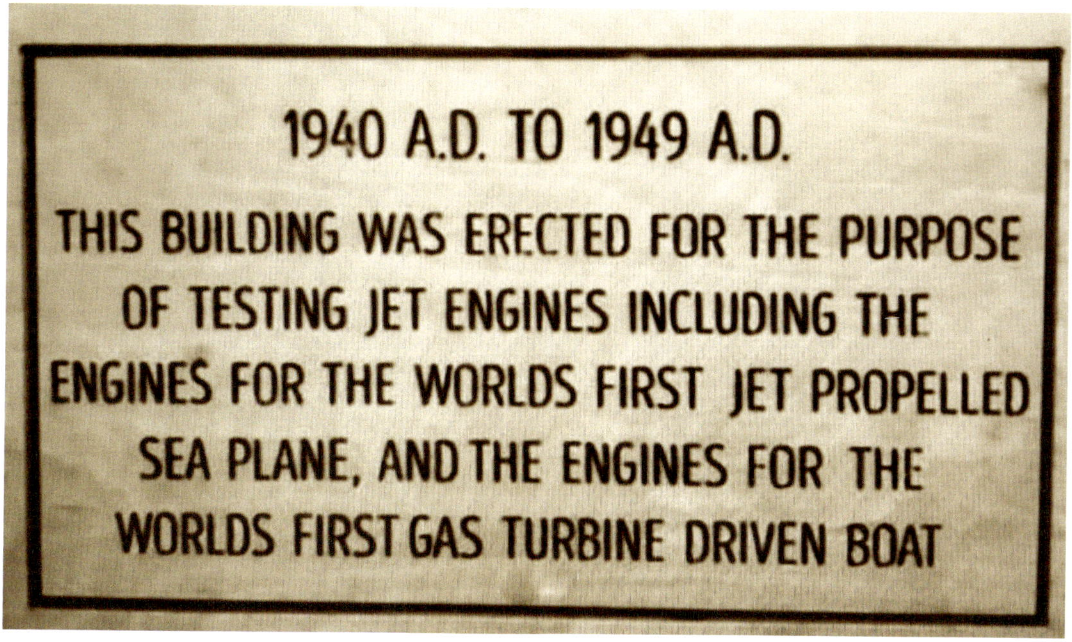

Stone plaque commemorating the work carried out in Wincham.

The first test flight took place in October 1941, and a Power Jets team and the engine were flown to the United States to enable General Electric to further develop the project. They worked quickly, and their XP-59A Airacomet was airborne by October 1942, before the RAF Meteor.

Both the Germans and the British had jet fighters in the last months of the war. The Germans had the first jet fighter, the Messerschmitt ME 262, entering service in 1944, and Britain had the Gloster Meteor, which also entered service in 1944, and was mainly used to take out V1 pilotless 'buzz bombs'.

Gary Olive from Wincham later leased the offices at the site in 2008 and bought a stone to commemorate the vital role that Wincham had played in the development of the jet engine. A special ceremony was held to commemorate the significant achievement. The plaque can now be found at the entrance of Wincham Community Centre. 'Now we have the stone on display as a reminder of the great engineering strides that were made right here in the village' said Councillor May at the ceremony.

As for Frank Whittle, he retired from the RAF in 1948 with the rank of air commodore and was knighted in the same year. He died on 9 August 1996.

HORNER'S CREAMERY AND LATER SKI YOGHURT

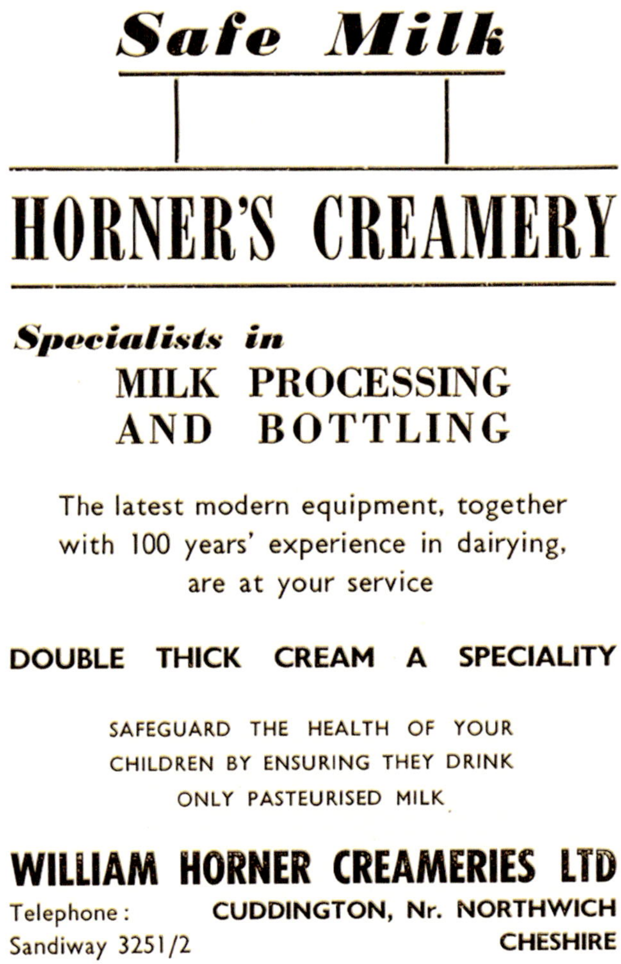

Horner's Creamery advert.

The former Nestlé Ski yoghurt factory in Cuddington has been redeveloped into a residential area. The 20-acre site was purchased for redevelopment, and the purchasers aimed to transform a long-standing eyesore into a valuable asset for the village. The factory closed in 2009, and plans were approved for a £40 million development including 156 new homes, allotments and public spaces.

However, let us examine the business from the beginning. (Source: Cheshire Live)

In 1827, a man was born in Grimethorpe, Yorkshire. Unlike many men from the village, he did not work down the pit. His name was William Horner. By 1871, he was living at No. 25 Onslow Road, Fairfield in Liverpool, and working as a cheese merchant. His wife died that year, and he was left to bring up their eight children. In 1877, he married Eliza Ellen Mountford, and by 1881, he was a cream, cheese and butter maker living at The Bryn, Cuddington.

The *Nantwich Guardian* of Saturday 13 July 1878 reported on a machine that would keep beer fresh. This also served as a milk cooler, ensuring the milk's freshness for much longer than was previously possible. The local agent for this miraculous machine was Mr Horner of the cheese factory in Weaverham near Northwich. At this time, the creamery was in Smith's Lane, Weaverham, off the High Street.

Soon after, they moved to a larger premises at Gorstage near Cuddington. In 1887, William Horner lost £2,500 (equivalent to £420,080.40 today). Clement Taylor, a money lender and stockbroker, had an office on Northwich High Street. Clement's CV was first class, having started work as a clerk in one of Northwich's banks, where he was held in high esteem. When setting up his own office, the rich and famous were soon drawn in with the promise of big dividends for their investment. He dealt mainly in shares relating to the Salt Union, and William Horner was one such investor, handing over £2,500 for shares in the Cheshire Salt Mining Company. The promise of big dividends continued to lure investors to Clement Taylor's door.

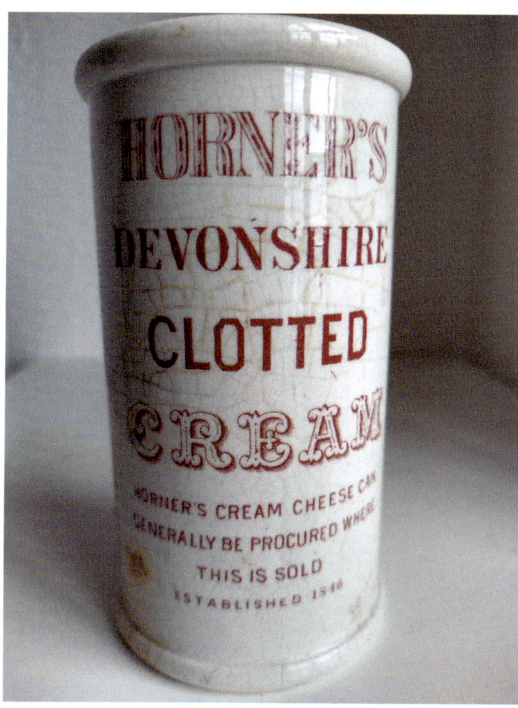

Horner's pot of Devonshire clotted cream. (Source: John Mears)

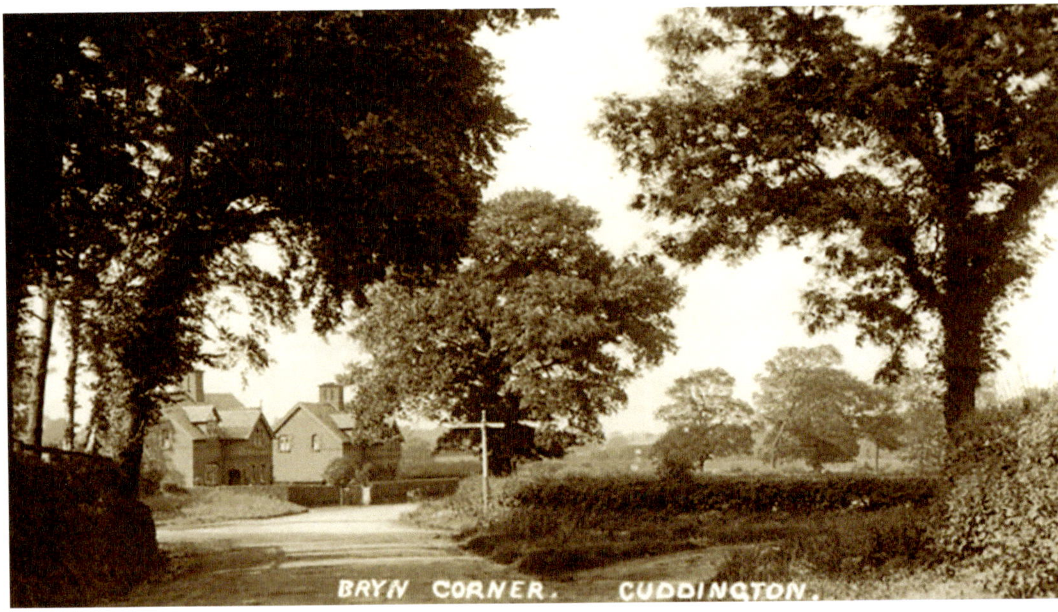

Bryn Corner, Cuddington.

Mr Taylor's clerk informed him that the business was failing. Soon after, Taylor left the office, making good his escape and disappeared with the money via Witton, now Northwich station. The heaviest loser was Mr William Horner of the Creameries, Cuddington.

By 1891, William still lived at The Bryn and was a cheese factor. In 1897, at the age of seventy, he died and was buried in Weaverham churchyard. The grave is seen opposite and includes the names of William and Ann Horner and George and Ada Horner.

One of William's sons, George Horner, born in 1866, went to school in Staffordshire. By 1891, he was living in the family home, The Bryn. By 1901, he was working for his brother at Whitchurch, where they had opened a second creamery in Prees. In 1903, he married his wife, Ada.

By 1910, George had returned to Cheshire and was a creamery proprietor living at Gorstage House, Weaverham. Ten years later, he is recorded as living in Groby Road, Altrincham, and later at Lumley House, Hough Green, Chester, and finally at 'Morrab', Kelsall Hill, where he died in February 1942. Five months later, his wife, Ada, died. The creamery, still known as William Horner Creameries Ltd, went from strength to strength, including milk deliveries throughout Mid Cheshire. The family became wealthy, as evidenced by their wills.

In the early 1960s, the *Winsford Chronicle* reported that a spokesman for the old-established firm, William Horner Creameries Ltd, would neither admit nor deny that it was in the process of selling the business to the giant Express Dairies company. At the time, the William Horner company had a big new factory building and was engaged in large-scale milk distribution, both retail and wholesale. It was the largest milk farm in the North West, producing a million bottles of milk per week and other dairy products, and employing about 250 people.

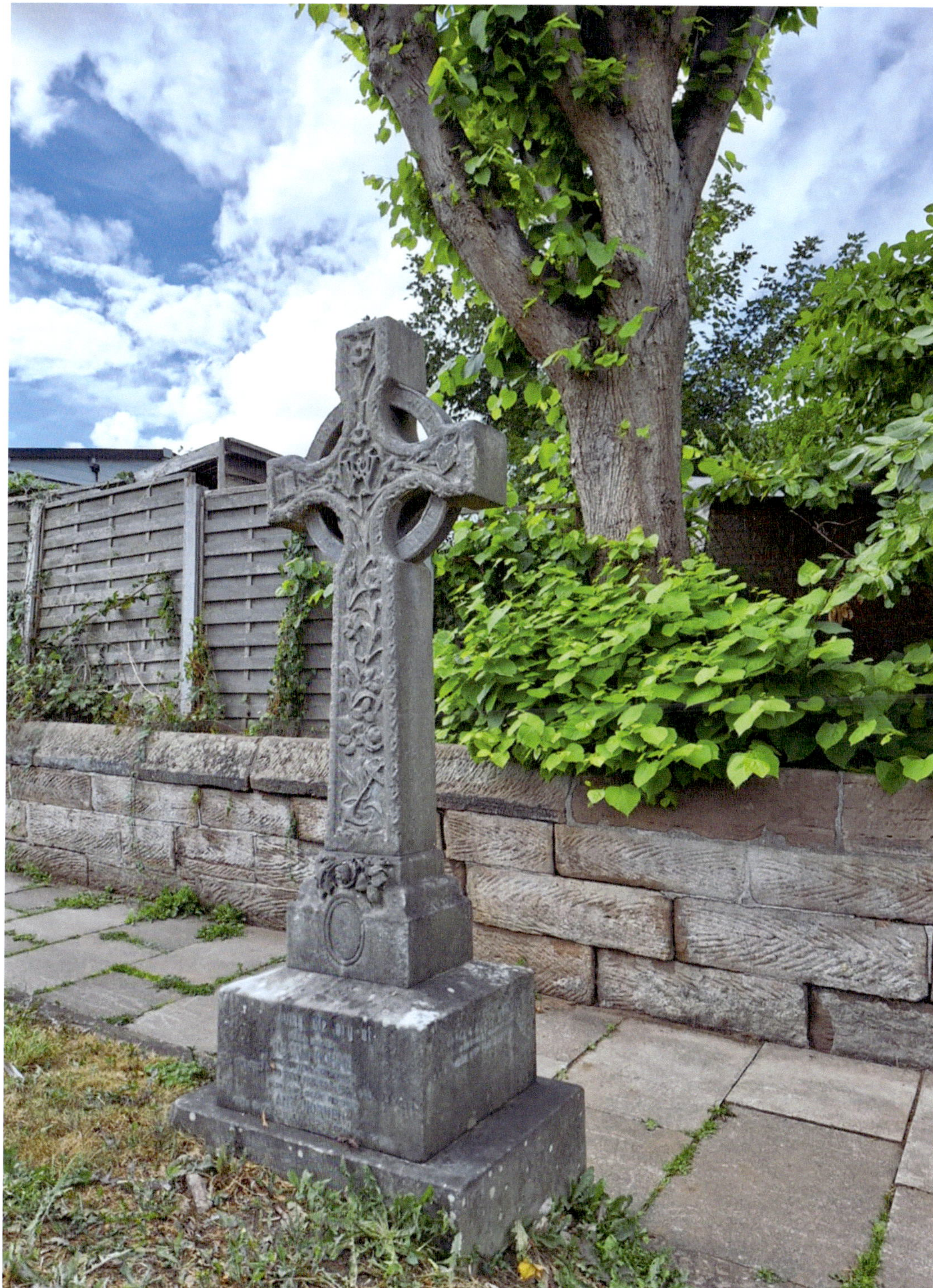

Horner's grave in Weaverham churchyard.

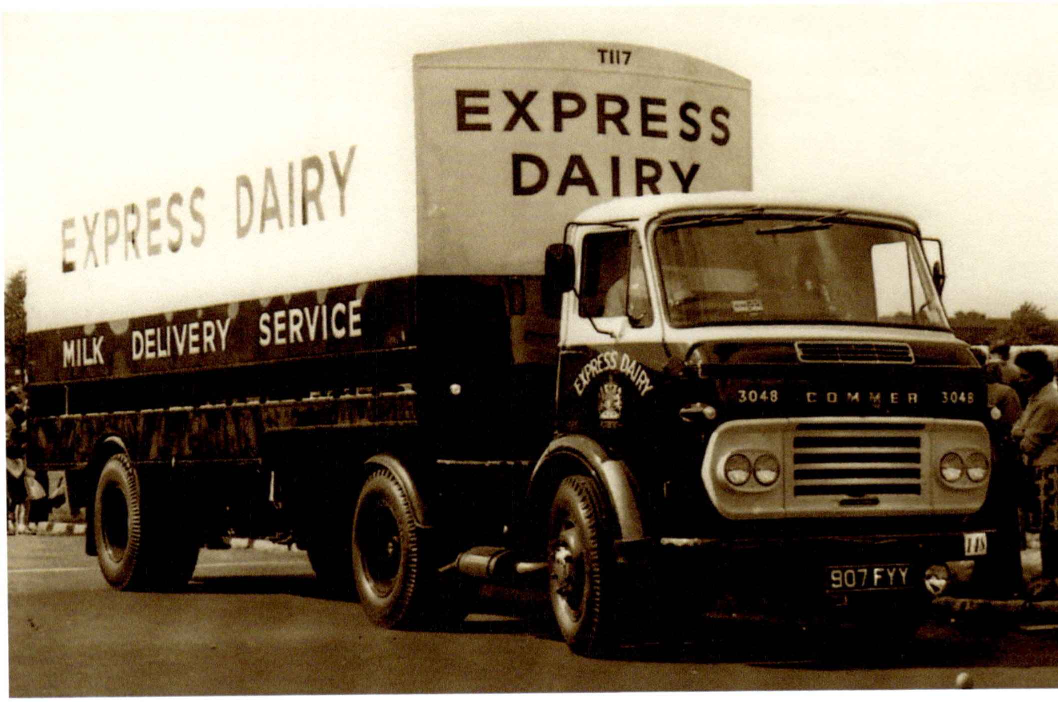

Express Dairy delivery lorry.

The rumours were true, and in 1963, Express Dairies bought the Horner company. Very soon after, they commenced specialising in yoghurt and its derivatives. By 2002, Express Dairies had become Northern Foods. They owned Ski Yoghurt and its derivatives, including the child-friendly Munch Bunch brand. They sold the business, including the Eden Vale and Cuddington yoghurt factory, to Nestlé. The factory retained the name Eden Vale, and it was later sold to developers.

The eyesore former Nestlé Ski factory, in Cuddington, is on the verge of being transformed after a planning application was submitted. The final plans for the area include the creation of 160 family homes, community allotments, new public open spaces and links to the 20-acre site on the northern edge of the village.

The derelict former yoghurt factory has been vacant since 2007, when Nestlé withdrew its operations to mainland Europe. In 2009, Ainscough Strategic Land acquired the site and has since been working closely with Cheshire West and Chester Council to redevelop it.

Nigel McGurk, managing director of Ainscough, said: 'The evolution of this planning application has been a brilliant example of real "localism" in practice. As well as working closely with the council, we have had an overwhelmingly positive response from the community and, in particular, ideas brought forward during consultation will now bring lasting benefits to Cuddington. The site has undergone eighteen months of consultation, and more than 300 people attended a public meeting held by developers in July this year, giving them the chance to put forward their own ideas for the site.' The residential area is now called The Eden Grange Estate as a nod to its history.

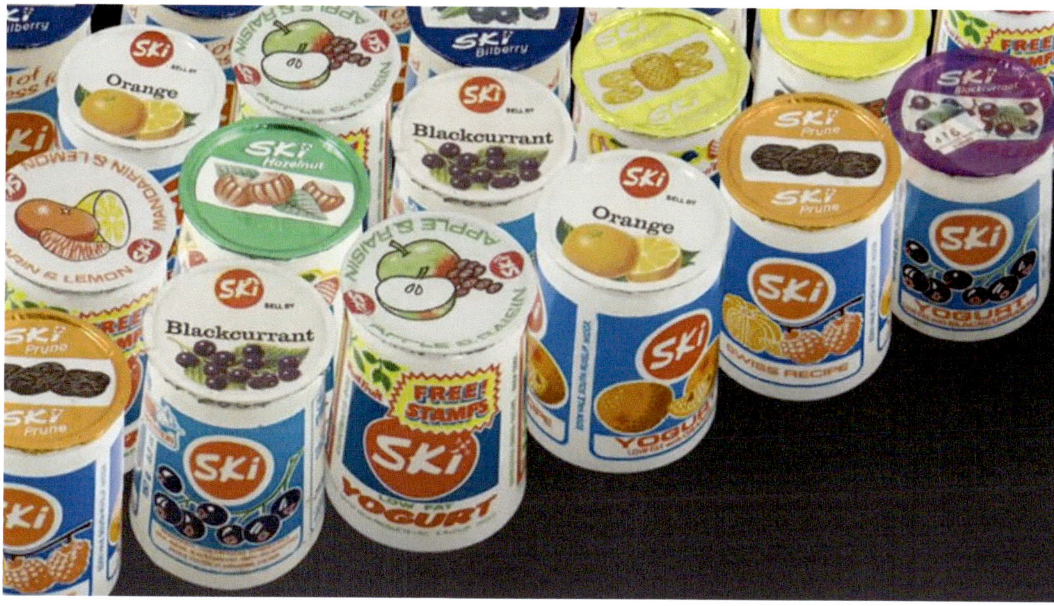

Ski Yoghurt advert.

MOORE AND BROCK

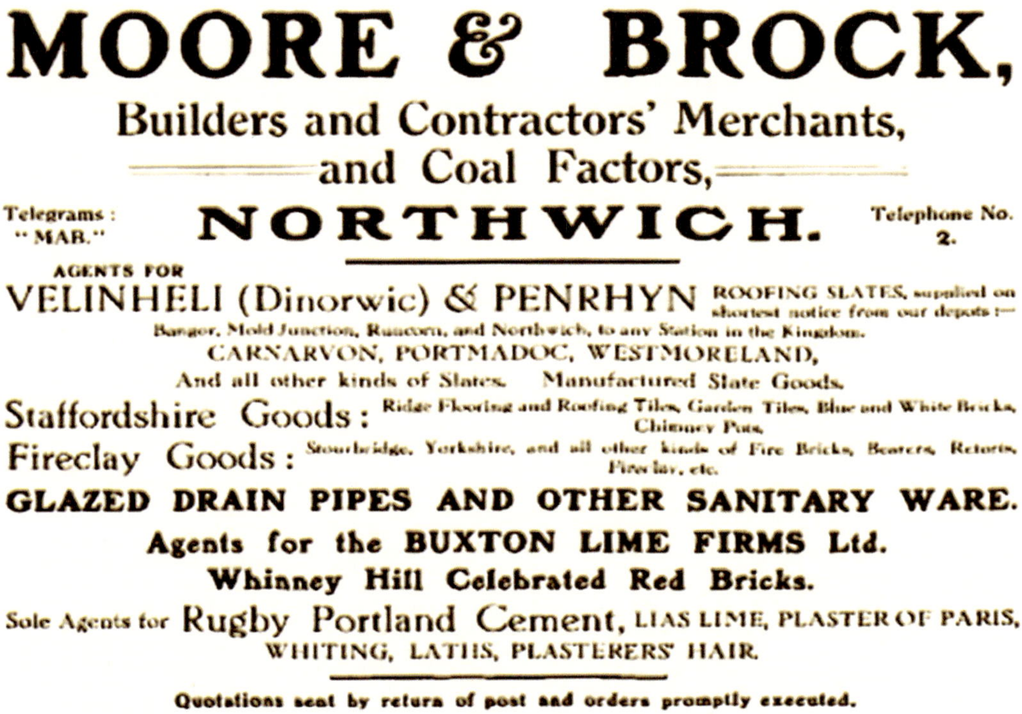

Moore and Brock advert.

Northwich Guardian, November 2008:

> Regeneration has taken another leap forward, with the start of the demolition of the old Moore and Brock buildings at Baron's Quay.
>
> The disused builder's warehouse will now free a key riverside area for Northwich Vision's Barons Quay development. Every part of the old warehouse will now be recycled following the 10-week demolition.
>
> Clr Arthur Wood, lead councillor for area working and regeneration, said: 'It is not only the bricks that will be reused. All hard standing, from concrete and masonry to the site's roads, will be crushed on site and used again.'
>
> Some of the buildings date back to 1834 and have more recently been used as the contractor's headquarters for the now-completed project to fill Northwich's abandoned salt mines.
>
> The former Grade Two listed building had fallen into disrepair and became unsafe following a fire at the site.

But what of its history before it became the foundation of the Barons Quay shopping and entertainment centre? The Northwich Carrying Company Ltd was formed in 1883 by local slate merchant Thomas Moore (1839–98) to carry goods between Northwich and Liverpool. The company was established to supply salt and chemicals to numerous small businesses and shopkeepers, as well as to Brunner Mond following its formation in 1874. In 1886, the company carried passengers from the Crown and Anchor yard at Northwich; their SS *Superb* departed Northwich twice weekly.

An early shareholder was W. J. Yarwood, who built and repaired several of their vessels at his shipbuilding company. Thomas Moore joined the business (note the name on the photograph of Moore's warehouse, J. Moore; we can find no J. Moore and assume it is a misprint).

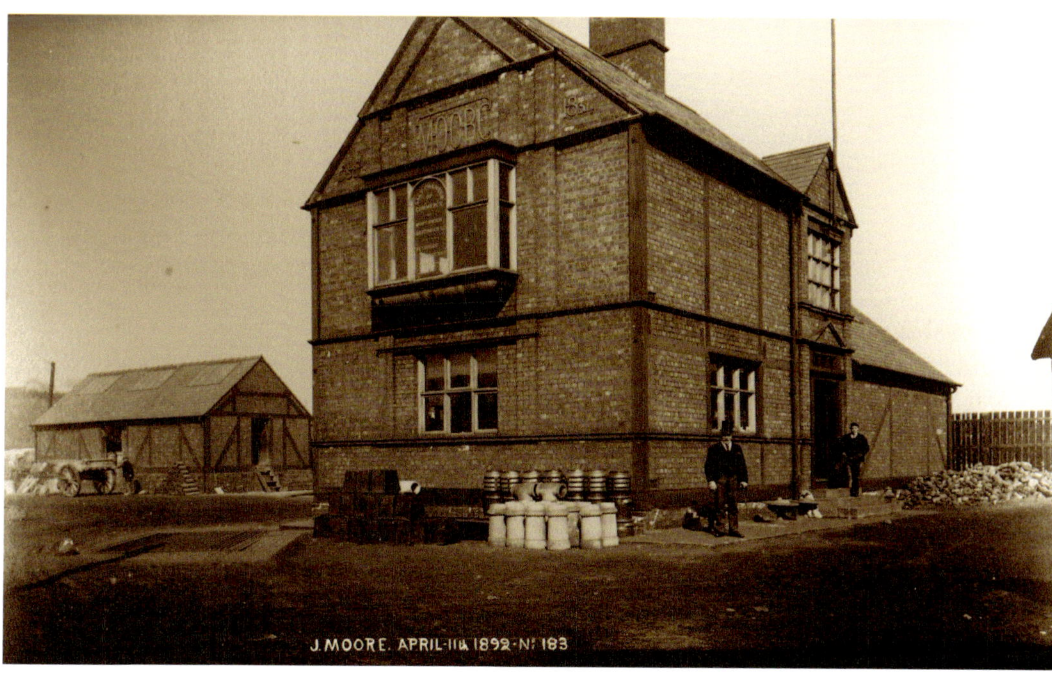

J. Moore building at Barons Quay, 1892.

In 1893, Thomas Moore was engaged in a rates war with the Weaver Navigation, but the following year, the Northwich Carrying Company announced that the difference had been settled. However, it revealed much about the Northwich Carrying Company, and the following year, the examination of Thomas Moore revealed much more about its business. The report from the Joint Select Committee of the House of Lords and the House of Commons, on Canal Rates, Tolls, and Charges Provisional Order Bills, together with the proceedings of the committee, minutes of evidence, and index, House of Commons Parliamentary Papers Publication Year 1894, was reported as follows:

> Mr THOMAS MOORE is called in, and, having been sworn, is examined, as follows:
> You are a Coal, Lime, Slate, and General Builders Merchant at Northwich?
> — I am.
> And you are also General Manager of the Northwich Carrying Company, Limited?
> — I am.
> When was that company formed?
> — About 11 years ago.
> Their premises are situated in Northwich, are they not?
> — Yes.
> Which way does the traffic of that company pass along the Weaver Navigation?
> — Entirely between Northwich and Liverpool along the Weaver
> What articles do you send along that route?
> — All descriptions of articles, everything from Class A to Class 5, and a large proportion of that is the chemicals ...

In 1906, George Henry Brock joined Thomas Moore as co-director in the business, which dealt in all forms of building materials from the large Barons Quay premises and yard. The business was very successful, both in the sales department and at the Northwich Carrying Company, and the name eventually changed to Moore and Brock. In 1898, Thomas Moore died at his home, Riversdale, Leftwich, and his son, also named Thomas, took his place. He, in turn, died at the Limes Nursing Home, Hough Green, Chester, on 30 April 1938, at the age of sixty-six.

In 1900, competition for the shipping arm of the business was losing out to road and rail. This was not helped by the sinking of their steamer *Alice Capper* in a collision in the Mersey. It had been built in 1875 by John Thompson (& Sons) of Northwich and was in collision with a lighter and sank in a few seconds. The crew of four on board were rescued. It had been carrying a cargo of flour, butter and laths, etc.

In 1920, the Penmaenmawr and Welsh Granite Company was planning to take over the Northwich Carrying Company, but the takeover never materialised. River transport was becoming less economically viable due to the challenge from road and rail, and the company was wound up in 1932. The Northwich Carrying Company name was sold for £5.

George Henry Brock of The Mount, Hartford, died on 6 March 1923, aged seventy-three. He is buried in Hartford church. Moore and Brock continued to serve the building trades through the years from their Barons Quay premises in Northwich. The company also had depots at Chester, The Quarry, Handbridge, Earle Street, Crewe, and a wallpaper shop in High Street, Northwich.

Business went well until 1990, when the mines beneath it – namely the Barons Quay, Witton Bank, Neuman's, and Penny's Lane – were causing concern due to potential subsidence. It was proposed that something would have to be done, and the site's value was drastically reduced. As a result, Moore and Brock ceased trading and the office and warehouse stood empty for some time. The premises were used to store the builders' materials for the coming work to stabilise the mines below.

In 2004, the old Vale Royal Borough Council was awarded £20 million to rectify the problem by removing millions of litres of brine and filling the voids with grout composed of pulverised fuel ash, cement and salt. This was mixed by Brunner Mond and pumped via a pipeline from the works and into the voids. It was the largest project of its kind in the world, and it succeeded. In 2006, the derelict four-storey Moore and Brock warehouse was burned down in mysterious, some say suspicious, circumstances; the building was listed. The English Partnerships Stabilisation project was completed, and the Barons Quay development was then built on the site.

BATES FOUNDRIES

A look now at the large Bates family and their iron foundry businesses in Northwich and Winsford.

William Bates was born in Sowerby Bridge, West Yorkshire, and moved to Northwich with his family around 1844. His sons, William Edwin, Henry, and James, were all to join him in his chosen occupation as a foundry owner. The primary industries of Northwich at that time were salt and boat building; these, plus the soon-to-be-established chemical industry, all required iron or brass fixtures. On arrival, William initially set up a foundry in the Cotton Works in Witton, Northwich. However, due to space constraints at Barons Quay, all three sons subsequently set up their own foundries. Henry started at H. Bates in Station Road, Witton; William Edwin at W. E. Bates in Leftwich; and James at J. Bates, New Road, Winsford.

A foundry had existed in Leftwich since the early 1800s. In 1821, the Eaton family company was dissolved due to debts, and in 1835, the foundry was put up for sale, with buildings, furnaces, a mill, a large yard, and a wharf of 40 yards on the River Weaver. At that time, it was in the possession of a Mr Stork. It is presumed that Thomas Dunn and John Johnson then took over, although this partnership ended abruptly only two years later. John Johnson continued alone until 1840, when the site was put up for auction by Mrs Johnson.

In 1867, William Edwin Bates decided to set up new premises and left the Cotton Works, Barons Quay (previously known as Cockshotts Mill), relocating to London Road, Leftwich. Interestingly, in 1869, a patent number was assigned, 3325, raised by William Edwin Bates and Thomas Dodd in respect of an invention that provided 'certain improvements in machinery or apparatus for cracking nuts'. It is not known if this device was successful!

By 1881, William Edwin employed upwards of thirty men and sixteen boys. He resided at No. 14 Dock Road, Leftwich, with his wife, Eliza, six sons and two daughters.

Of note was a marine steam engine built in 1885 by W. E. Bates & Sons, fitted into the iron screw steamer *Bengal*. The engine was built for Joseph Verdin & Sons, a local salt magnate, who used many steamers to transport salt from his mines in Northwich, and later Winsford, to Liverpool Docks along the River Weaver. Engines of this type were fitted to many types of barges, salt flats and small coastal vessels. The 'Bengal engine' is now on display at the Ellesmere Port boat museum.

By the 1911 census, William Edwin Sr was a widower, had retired, and was living at 'Elmcot', Rocky Lane, Heswall, on the Wirral. He died just two years later, aged seventy-eight, in

July 1913, leaving his sons, Nathaniel and Albert, £6,758 in his will. This would be worth approximately £678,000 in 2025.

In 1921, Oswald Bates, another son, was living at No. 55 Church Road, Northwich, and was listed as retired, having worked at W. E. Bates. In 1942, the Leftwich foundry was still in the hands of a Bates family member, William Edwin's grandson/son, and J. Allder Bates, a partner. Shortly afterwards, the foundry was acquired by Brunner Mond. It was reported in 1963 that it was no longer functioning.

WITTON – H. BATES & SONS FOUNDRY

Henry Bates moved from the existing Cotton Works Foundry to Station Road, Witton, in the early 1860s and was also the licensee of the Cock Hotel from 1860 to 1864. He built the iron and brass foundry in about 1864. His foundry at that time was moulding and casting pipes for the local chemical industry, and he began in the yard of the Cock Hotel but soon moved to the opposite side and opened the foundry.

At this time, there were only a handful of employees; however, by the early 1900s, it had risen to sixty. Henry was a quiet and unassuming man, and for many years, he was the captain of the Witton Fire Brigade and constable of Witton-cum-Twambrooks.

Henry Bates retired from the foundry in 1896 and handed the business over to his sons.

In 1911, William Henry Bates, the son of Henry Bates, was working at the H. Bates foundry in Station Road, Northwich, and living with his wife, shown as the innkeeper, at the Farmers Arms in Middlewich Road, Rudheath.

In 1912, Henry Bates died at the age of eighty-seven. He had been living at Parkdale, No. 140 Middlewich Road, Northwich, a house built for the Bates family in 1892. He left £8,500 in

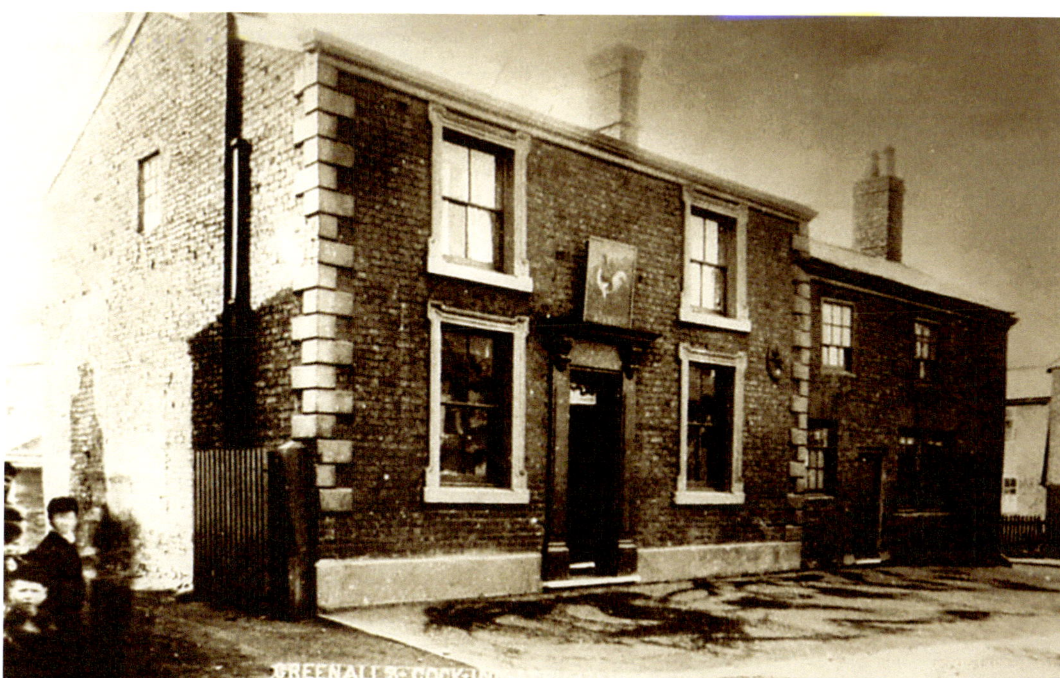

Cock Hotel, Witton Street, Northwich.

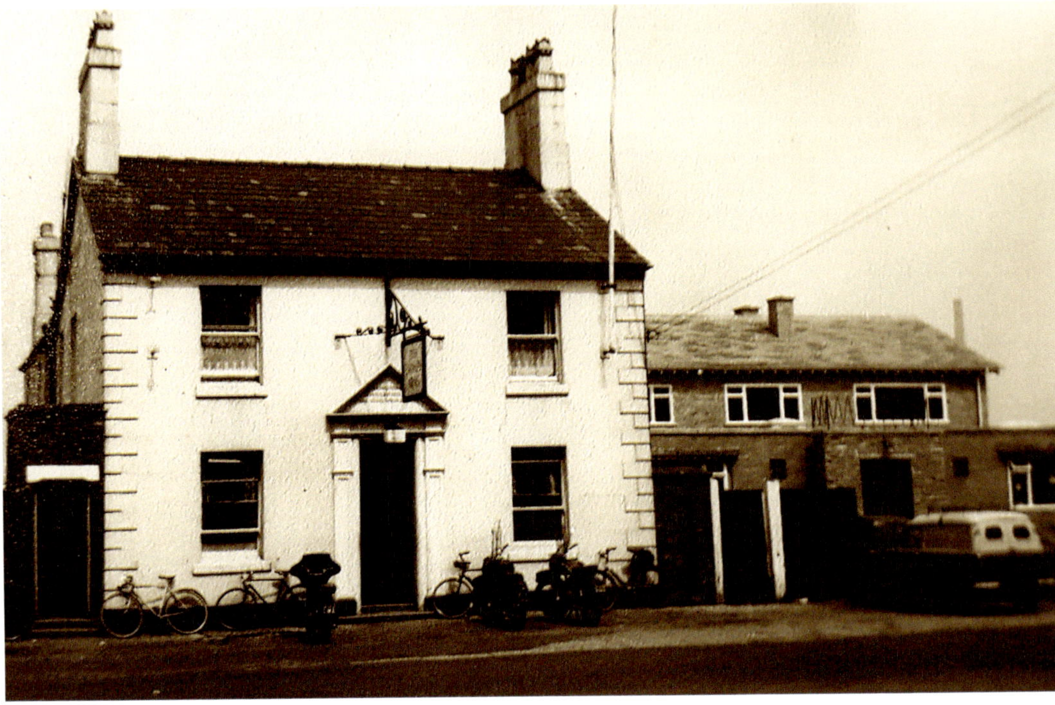

Old Farmers Arms, Rudheath.

his will, today worth around £844,000, to Charles Tarbuck Bates (an iron founder) and Edwin Bates (an engineer).

The last of Henry Bates' sons, Joseph, died in 1940 at seventy-two; however, by then, the next generation had already taken over the firm. The main business, as reported in 1963, was primarily making pipes for the chemical industry, specifically for ICI, and Bates's work could be found all over the world. They also provided ironwork for the Mid and South Cheshire Water Board.

In 1974, a newspaper article mentioned that due to the failing economy at the time, the Bates foundry in Station Road was suffering from shortages of fuel, materials, and, most importantly, labour. Mr Bates stated that the iron foundry business was a rapidly declining industry and it was difficult to recruit experienced men. At that time, there were twenty-eight employees.

Plans were put forward in 1979 to the then-named Vale Royal District Council to regenerate the land where the H. Bates foundry had been for retail warehousing. This didn't happen immediately; the H. Bates & Sons foundry reportedly closed in 1984, and development of the land followed.

J. BATES, WINSFORD

The third foundry set up by the Bates brothers is by James Bates in New Road, Winsford. James was born in Sowerby Bridge in 1824. He was living in Winnington Hill, Northwich, in 1851, but by 1861, he was in Over, Winsford. Although exact details are long since lost to history, his son Arthur was born at Foundry House, New Road, Winsford, in 1858. Therefore, it is likely that the foundry was set up between 1851 and 1858, laying the foundations for a prosperous and long-lasting business. James' son, Arthur, was groomed to take over the business, which he did after his father died in 1901, aged seventy-eight, leaving £6,176 (£660,000 today) to his wife and a local ironmonger, Richard Chesters.

Keeping with the family tradition, Arthur's two sons, William Geoffrey and Albert Herd, also joined the company, and when Arthur retired in about 1918 and became just the figurehead of the company, they took over the helm to run the foundry. The firm had a considerable presence in both domestic and international trade, and it is reputed that almost all the equipment for brine pumping in the Winsford salt mines was made there. The family lived on Swanlow Lane, Winsford, for the latter part of the 1800s, and later at Darnhall Cottage on Darnhall School Lane, Winsford.

In 1926, James' son Arthur died at the age of seventy-eight, leaving £6,071 to his wife and sons. The amount would be the equivalent of £323,000 today.

The company continued to be successful, and in 1946, advertisements for boilers and central heating equipment began appearing for the general public to purchase. The foundry in New Road had been operating for almost 100 years when it was closed in 1954. It relocated to land at the top of Wharton Hill next to the Over & Wharton railway station. The new building consisted of a moulding shop three times the size of the old one, and the 2.5-acre site also housed a machine shop, a pattern shop and a canteen. In all, the new foundry was to provide a 150 per cent increase in production capacity. Following a deadlock in pay and productivity discussions in 1977, the foundry was likely to have to close. At that time, fifteen employees were affected, and recruiting suitably skilled workers was complex. In 1978, all the foundry's equipment was sold at auction, although retirement was cited as the reason. By 1979, the site was occupied by Whitehurst Transport Limited, which manufactured packing cases, pallets, laboratory furniture and light haulage. The foundry, which had been in business for almost 120 years, was no more.

NORTHWICH BREWERIES

In 1880, James Hampson was a wholesale brewer with a brewery in Witton Street; another brewer in the same street was Nash and Skidmore. By 1896, both had gone, and James Hampson's premises were purchased by N. P. Sandiford and Son, which remained there until the 1970s.

Their main business was the manufacture of mineral waters and the sale of wines and spirits. They also bottled and sold beer for other breweries, particularly Bass in Burton upon Trent.

The company also had a branch in Manchester. Sandifords were well known in Northwich; opening in 1896, their stone and glass pop bottles were delivered to the door.

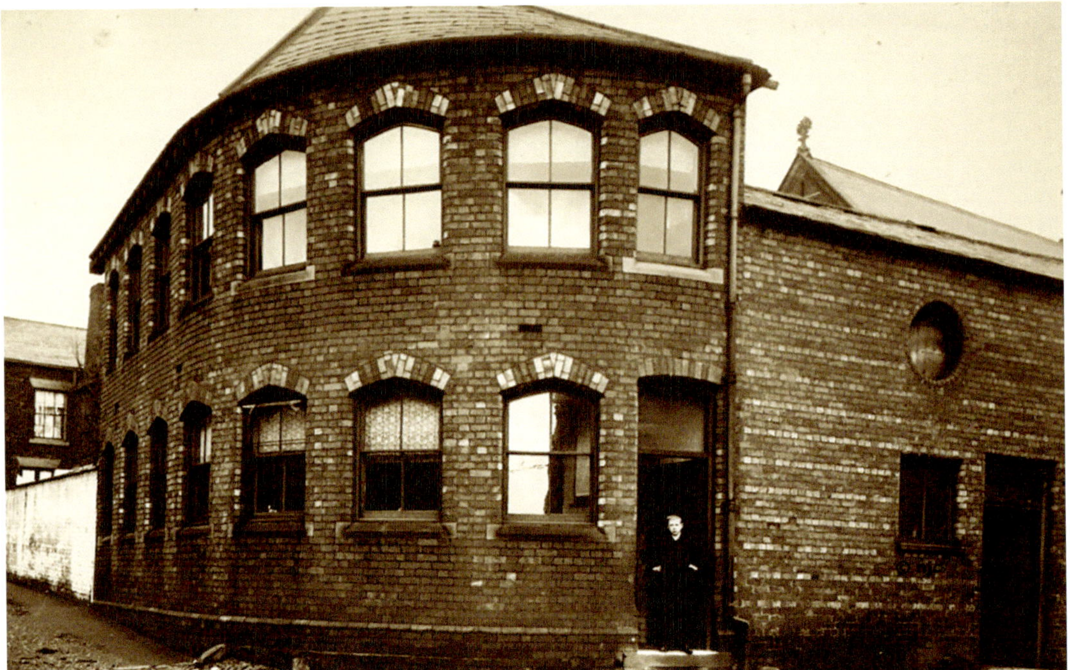

Sandifords Brewery, 1895.

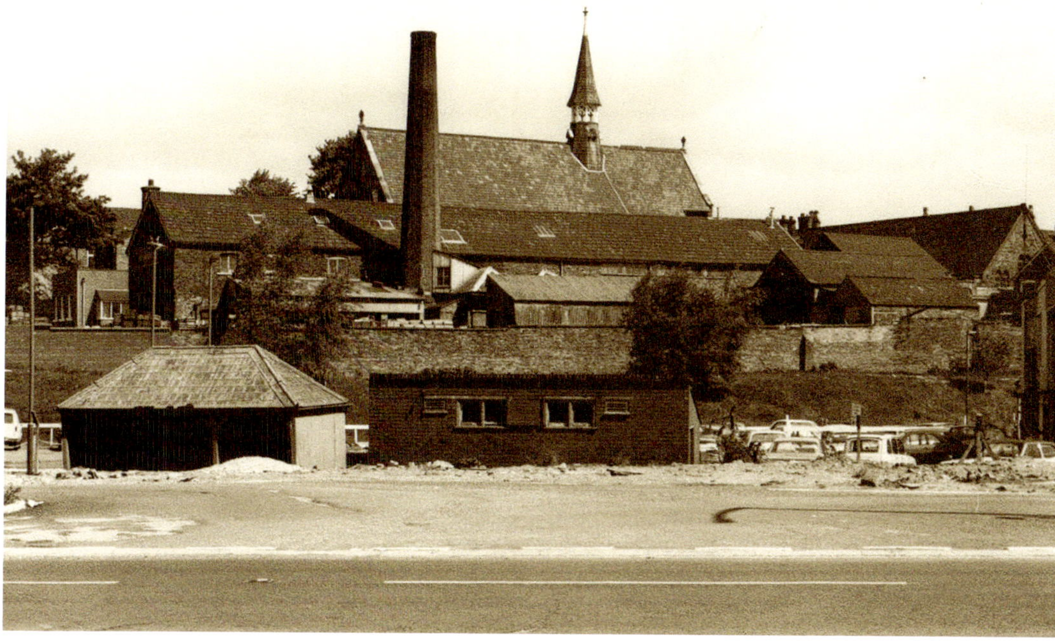

Sandifords Brewery, *c.* 1960s.

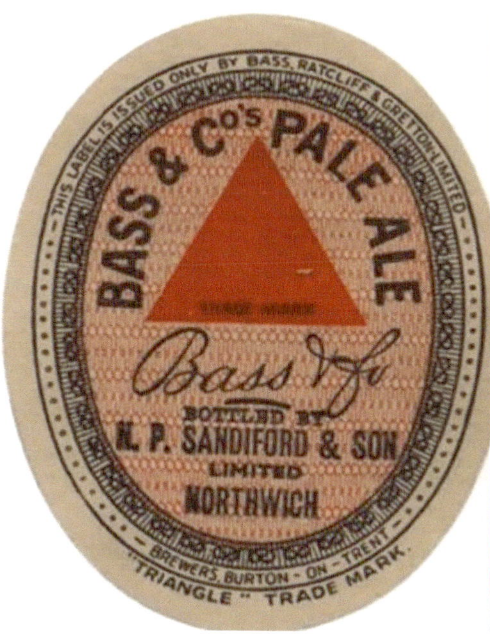

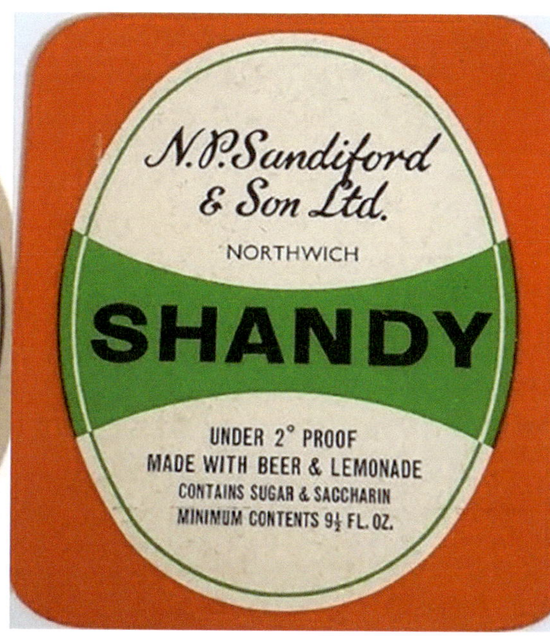

Sandifords bottle label and beer mat.

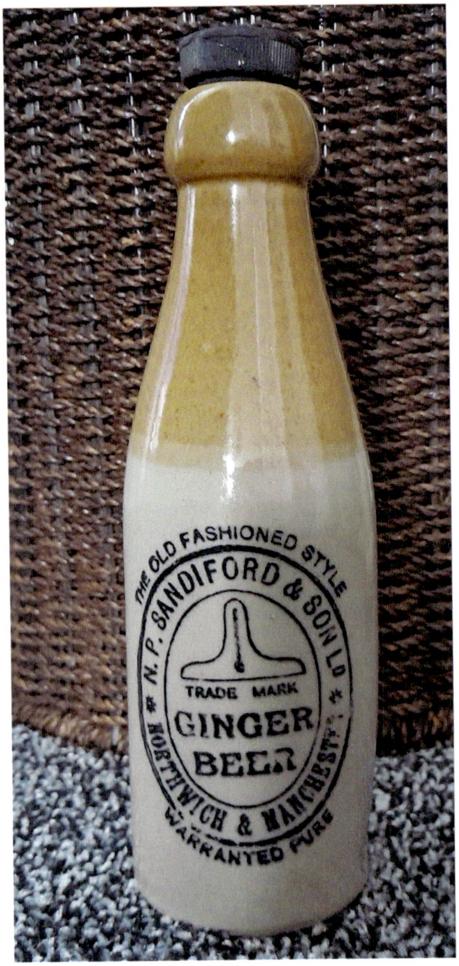

Sandifords bottle.

***

That is a brief look at some of the past industries that have served the people and tradespeople of Northwich and its surroundings, and, in some cases, around the world. Not many towns the size of Northwich could boast two shipbuilders providing small warships, tugboats, canal boats and river craft. A large family that provided all the start-up capital for their own engineering companies and went on to complete an impressive number of prestigious engineering works, including involvement in the manufacture of the Mulberry Harbours towed to the French coast during the Second World War.

Mention of the huge chemical company Brunner Mond/ICI cannot be missed. For many years they dominated the world of chemical excellence. Their portfolio included the invention of polythene, now frowned upon due to the dislike of plastic debris that pervades our shores, green spaces and public areas. But better is done with the stuff than the criticism suggests. At least Brunner Mond warned the government not to use one of its disused factories for the TNT work. The government disagreed due to the war effort and blew up a big lump of London!

ABOUT THE AUTHORS

Paul Hurley has been a freelance writer since retiring from the police in 2002 and has been writing professionally ever since. Paul has amassed a CV that includes several magazine articles and credits in local and national newspapers. He has written numerous books for Amberley Publishing on the history of Cheshire, as well as railways and other topics. He has also produced an autobiography and an award-winning novel. He lives in Winsford with his wife, Rose, and his hobbies include writing, travelling and classic cars.

Rose Hurley is an expert in family and local history research. This is her third book with her husband, published by Amberley Publishing, and follows the successful publication of *Cheshire Murders and Misdemeanours* and *Tragic Cheshire*. Prior to her recent retirement, she was a senior IT manager, and her current interests are writing, travelling and walking.

Books by the same authors:

Fiction
Britain Invaded

Non-Fiction:
The Good, the Bad and the Crafty (autobiography)
Middlewich (with Brian Curzon)
Middlewich and Holmes Chapel Through Time
Winsford Through Time
Villages of Mid Cheshire Through Time
Villages of Mid Cheshire Through Time (2nd edition)
Frodsham and Helsby Through Time
Nantwich Through Time
Nantwich History Tour
Middlewich & Holmes Chapel Through Time
Sandbach, Wheelock & District Through Time
Knutsford & District Through Time
Knutsford History Tour
Northwich Through Time
Northwich Through the Ages
Northwich History Tour
Northwich, Winsford & Middlewich Through Time
Chester Through Time (with Len Morgan)
Chester in the 1950s
Chester in the 1960s
Chester History Tour
Chester Pubs
Chester Reflections
Chester History Tour
Chester Pubs (with Len Morgan)
Chester in 50 Buildings
Cheshire with Historic England
Brewing in Cheshire
Cheshire Through Time

Macclesfield Through Time
Macclesfield History Tour
Steam Nostalgia in the North of England (with Phil Braithwaite)
A–Z of Crewe
Remembering Steam (hardback) (with Phil Braithwaite)
Remembering Steam (paperback)
Remembering Steam (3rd edition)
The Changing Railways of Britain (hardback) (with Phil Braithwaite)
The Big Four (hardback) (with Jeremy Suter)
Sir William A Stanier FRS (with Phil Braithwaite)
Cheshire Murders and Misdemeanours (with Rose Hurley)
Tragic Cheshire (with Rose Hurley)
Blitz on Cheshire (with Rose Hurley)